DRESSAGE
FORMULA

DRESSAGE FORMULA

Third Edition

ERIK HERBERMANN

Foreword by Egon von Neindorff

J. A. Allen
London

British Library Cataloguing in Publication Data
A catalogue record for this book is available from the British Library

First edition published 1980
Reprinted 1984
Reprinted 1986
Second edition, completely revised and re-set, published 1989
Reprinted 1993
Third edition, completely revised and re-set, published 1999

Published in Great Britain by
J.A. Allen & Company Limited
1 Lower Grosvenor Place
London SW1W OEL

ISBN 0.85131.753.7

Design by Judy Linard
Typeset by Textype Typesetters, Cambridge
Printed in Hong Kong by Dah Hua International Printing Press Co. Ltd.

In dedication to furthering equestrian ideals
based on the nature of the horse

Enter
the sanctuary of the horse
ever
with honour and respect

Contents

Vorwort

(foreword to the first edition)

Herr Erik Herbermann hat in sein mehrjärigen Aufenthalten an meinem Karlsruher Institut nicht nur reiterliches Können gezeigt. In einer Zeit des schnellen Wechsels und ständiger 'Umwertung der Werte' bewies Herbermann Klarheit und ungewönliches Einfühlungsvermögen mit der Beständigkeit, die seine Arbeitsweise auszeichnet. Das kam der erfreulichen Fülle fachlicher Kenntniss und praktischer Erfahrung sehr zugute, die in seinem Buch niedergelegt sind.

Die anschauliche Art der Darstellung, erläutert mit vielen instruktiven Bildaufnahmen aus der Arbeit des Autors, spricht den Leser als Freund der gemeinsamen Sache ebenso an wie die Probleme der täglichen Praxis. Sorgsamer Aufbau der Ausbildung von Pferd und Reiter ist der Grundzug dieses Bekenntnisses zur reellen, dauerhaften und vielseitigen Basis reiterlicher Erfolge.

So wünsche ich diesem Buch weite Verbreitung bei allen, denen die Probleme der Reiterei unserer Zeit mit Ernst am Herzen Liegen.

EGON VON NEINDORF

(Translation)

During his many years stay at my Riding Institution in Karlsruhe, Mr. Erik Herbermann has not only displayed equestrian ability. In an age of rapid changes and continual 'revaluation of values', Herbermann demonstrated a clarity and unusual perception for constancy which distinguish his method of work. This has come to good stead in the gratifying abundance of professional knowledge and practical experience which have been laid down in his book.

The attractive mode of presentation, which is illustrated by many instructive photographs of the author's work, relates to the reader as friend in both general matters as well as the problems of daily practice. Careful construction in the training of horse and rider is the characteristic of this Creed for a real, enduring and diverse basis of equestrian success.

Thus I wish this book a wide propagation to all those who seriously take to heart the problems of riding in our times.

EGON VON NEINDORFF

Preface

(to the First Edition)

This book contains an organized documentation of ideals and standards of fundamental academic dressage riding. It is a summary of my findings, based on a meticulous and critical study of the long-established principles of horsemanship, which I have diligently attempted to apply in both training and teaching.

This work does not pretend to be a replacement for the excellent literature written by the Great Masters. The basic concept is by no means new. The reason for this book is primarily to be a concise theoretical support: as a preparation for instruction, or for one's daily riding sessions, leaving these free to be fully utilized for their rightful purpose – the translation of theory into practice.

The emphasis of the text is singularly aimed at accuracy, brevity, clarity and objectivity. The headings of all sections are numbered for the purpose of cross-referencing, to avoid tedious repetition or redundancy.

Preface to the Third Edition

The goals set forth in the preface to the first edition of *Dressage Formula* remain uncompromisingly valid for this new, fully revised third edition. However, although the equestrian principles remain ever steady and true, rooted as they are in the horse's nature, the ways in which they can be described are indeed diverse. It is with this in mind that a face-lift has been given to this book, which has been so gratifyingly well received since it first appeared over eighteen years ago. In many ways, both obvious and subtle, the expression of the text in general has been improved in an attempt to achieve yet greater detail and clarity. The additions or alterations find their origin in notes spawned during the intervening years of teaching. However, because of the bulk of the material gathered, and because I wanted to stay true to the original 'concise note' format, several longer, 'prose-style' chapters which appeared in the second edition have been removed.

To facilitate a more direct access to material, the *Contents List* now includes cross-reference numbers as well as page numbering. Within the text, these cross-reference numbers appear against the sub-headings to which they relate. A comprehensive *Index* has also been added. Furthermore, to underscore key concepts and attitudes, some chapters now start with thumb-nail sketches, which I have called 'essences', 'guidelines', or 'concepts', and some also include a general introduction.

It is my sincere wish that this book will continue to serve as an avenue to deeper understanding and appreciation of this most marvellous of creatures, and that it should assist all who read it to discover the rich joyfulness that genuine harmony with the horse can bring to our lives. Above all, it is my wish that it may inspire an awareness that it is not only possible, but essential, that this exquisite harmony, which each of us so deeply hopes for, should be achieved with gentleness, intelligence and a kind heart towards the horse; because it is surely only through an honest and dignified approach that the fragile beauty of true horsemanship can be brought forth, enriching all with its delightful blossoms. Let's study the horse together.

ERIK F. HERBERMANN
Gambrills, Maryland, February 1999

Acknowledgments

I would like to thank my instructors and friends who over the years have contributed significantly to my education both as a person and as a horseman. I wish to include special recognition to those who have generously spent many hours of guidance, especially at the time when I could hardly have been considered anything other than a stumbling beginner. Often such individuals are overlooked only because they happen not to be among the ranks of 'world-renowned masters'.

Those who have contributed most significantly are: Mrs. Patricia Salt, FBHS, who taught, with precision and correctness, the art of riding that she herself had learned at the Spanish Riding School, and from her studies with Richard L. Wätjen. Others who assisted during these early years are Heidi Hannibal and Monty Smith. Further, it was through Dietrich von Hopffgarten that I was accepted as a working pupil at the Reitinstitut von Neindorff in Karlsruhe, Germany. I was greatly influenced by Mr von Hopffgarten's riding, which he demonstrated during several clinics which I attended, and I am most grateful to him for his contribution of explicit examples of fine horsemanship which radiated such undeniable qualities of competence and truth.

I am particularly deeply indebted to Herr Egon von Neindorff, from whom I have been able to glean the bulk of material upon which I have built my early equestrian experiences. It has been a unique and rich education to have worked under the guidance of this knowledgeable, artistic Master.

I wish to express my appreciation to Mr. John Pullen (second edition), and Mrs. Susan Dummit (third edition) for advice and feedback given.

Two deceased friends, whom I dearly loved and regarded most highly both as human beings and as horsemen, will not be forgotten: Walter B. Thiessen, and Dan A. A'haroni. My life and my horsemanship have been much enriched by having known them.

All photographs representing the author's work were taken by George A. Ross; this includes the cover picture. The X-ray photos were made possible through the kind assistance of Mr. and Mrs. Kenneth Giles, and were taken by Janice Kneider, and Dr. N. Brown, Chief Radiologist.

The photograph of the ballerina, Galina Samsova, is reproduced by the kind permission of Anthony Crickmay, and is from his book *Dancers* published by William Collins.

The photographs of Richard L. Wätjen and Oberbereiter Meixner are from Richard Wätjen's book *Dressage Riding*, and are reproduced by permission of the publishers, J. A. Allen & Co.

The photograph of Ernst Linderbauer is from the book *The Spanish Riding School of Vienna*, by Colonel Alois Podhajsky, published in Vienna in 1964.

Leonardo da Vinci's drawing *The Apostle Philip*, from the Royal Collection at Windsor Castle, has been reproduced through the gracious consent of Her Majesty Queen Elizabeth II. This sketch is from Leonardo's studies for his famous fresco, *The Last Supper*.

Finally, I wish to thank Mr. Joseph A. Allen, Mrs. Caroline Burt, Chief Executive, and the professionals of J. A. Allen & Co., for the special care they have taken to produce this third edition of *Dressage Formula* so beautifully.

001 *A Definition of Dressage*

Dressage is a methodical training of the horse. It is based on the three natural gaits – walk, trot and canter – which must be carefully cultivated and improved through structured gymnastic work. With this training the horseman attempts, while working the horse under saddle, to condition the horse to being ridden without in any way diminishing its nature. Thus balanced beauty and harmonious movement become possible, because all forms of exercises, regardless of difficulty, including the High School airs above the ground, find their roots in the same movements which the horse can already do in raw form in nature.

When correctly implemented, a solid foundation in basic dressage is useful for horses of all equestrian disciplines, being a practical gymnastic preparation which prolongs the creature's usefulness, and makes it a pleasure to ride.

SYNONYMS for the word 'DRESSAGE'

— Work on the flat (this term used in jumping)
— English riding
— Training by the Natural Method
— Academic riding (encompasses the next two disciplines)
— High School riding (advanced work)
— The art of Classical riding (dressage in its ultimate form)

An Introduction to the Horses in this Book

The horses that have been used to illustrate the text are all of the common 'back-yard' variety. The different breeds represented vary considerably in size, conformation, movement and temperament. Horses that have naturally good gaits, and which are naturally well balanced, offer the rider a great deal, and lessen the training problems substantially. For the rider who is capable, however, it is always interesting to work with equine material which is far from ideal, and carefully construct an end-product which is both pleasing to ride and to observe. When the basic motion of horses such as these can be improved, it stands as an irrefutable witness to the validity of effective practical gymnastics.

Atlantis

Grey gelding. Percheron–Thoroughbred cross. 16.1 hh. By nature a poor mover, with 'klunky' gaits. Retraining this fellow to become active, supple and obedient was like schooling a heavyweight wrestler to do ballet! Since he is a strong-minded, self-willed horse, it proved to be a challenging task. Atlantis started his training with the author at the age of 10. He was previously used as a family 'hack', and was occasionally hunted.

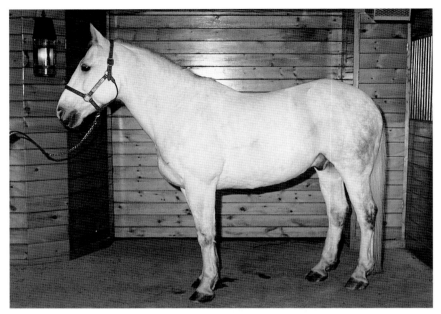

Atlantis.

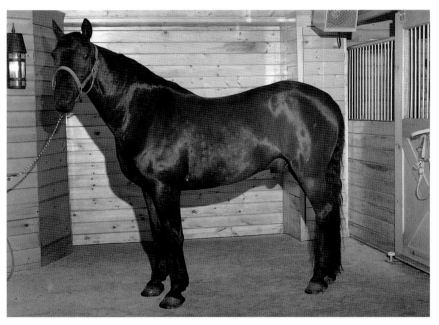

Meteorite.

Meteorite

Dark brown gelding. Standardbred cross (?). 15.3 hh. Before being purchased by the author he had gone the 'severe-bit route', and was quite thoroughly ruined. His mind and body were knotted with tensions. It took over two years to partially resolve the problems. This horse is represented in the book to demonstrate the interesting and valuable examples of how tensions manifest themselves in the gaits. He is by far the most athletic mover of these horses.

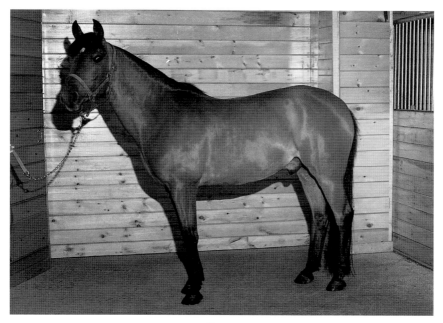

Barty.

Hawthorn's Bargel (Barty)

Bay gelding ¼ Arab − ¼ pony. 14.2 hh. He has a flat 'daisy-cutter' motion, with a dash of the choppy pony gait added. His jaw/throat/ jowl area is tight and fleshy, therefore the 'forward and down' exercises are demonstrated with him (these being excellent exercises for horses with this particular conformation problem.) He is a very willing little chap!

The Author with Atlantis.

CHAPTER I

The Mental Preparation
of the Rider

Essence

Riding is about:

— respect for, and love of, the horse
— trust–loyalty–friendship
— incorruptible commitment to the horse's well-bring
— coming to an understanding of the nature of the horse
— enhancing the horse's beauty through gymnastic work
— enjoying a harmonious partnership
— an avenue to self–awareness; self–improvement.

Our tasks are:

— to be the leader of the partnership
— to know that 'the buck stops here' …[1]
— to have clarity of purpose
— to work within the horse's, and our own, capabilities
— to utilize praise and correction; punishing *extremely* rarely
— to be thoughtful, patient, kind in all interaction with the horse.

[1] … exclusively with the rider. 'Management' is always solely responsible for finding viable solutions to *all* problems.

002 What Does the Riding Task Entail?

The horse already knows how to be a horse. The task of horsemanship lies   entirely with the rider. Through training, meaning the conditioning of the horse, the rider assists the horse to understand its role, that is, how to follow thoughtful leadership, and to develop its athletic potential which, over the years, gradually forms the horse's 'raw material' into a living work of art. This can only be achieved correctly through implementing well-structured gymnastic work which is in harmony with the horse's nature. In this way the rider gains access to the creature's willing compliance, which makes it possible to guide it easily and accurately under saddle through all the various movements which it can already perform naturally.

Besides becoming adept in the technical administration of the aids, the only physical responsibility to be mastered by the rider is, through the balanced harmony of a correct seat and position, to become an entirely inseparable part of the horse, in no way disturbing or impeding the freedom of its body motion.

In summary, it is the primary duty of the horseman to be strictly a 'control centre', not a physical mover, shover, or pusher-puller of the animal. This state can only come about when, through consistent use of the aids, the rider establishes a system of communication through which the horse comprehends what is wanted, and willingly moves its own body in compliance with the rider's requests.

003 Why the Many Years to Learn Correct Riding?

Riding is like an intangible phantom. Its living, dynamic properties can not be measured or weighed. Though there are certain technicalities to be mastered, horsemanship is a task directed mainly by elusive 'feel'. Two living creatures, each on entirely different physical and mental planes, attempt to become united. The unique character of each horse and personality of each rider, compounded by their own individual physical variations and challenges, comprise almost limitless combinations that must be dealt with in order to construct an end result in which the rider's mind does the thinking, and the horse's body does the doing.

While developing sufficient understanding and expertise, and so as to avoid the senselessness of trying to re-invent the wheel, we should adhere closely to the theoretical guidelines established by the great Masters over the past four centuries. It is important to realize, however, that the application of any theory is usually dependent on a host of attendant conditions, and often only brings desired results when practised patiently and correctly over an extended period.

The inevitable difficulties of misinterpretation of theory can only be overcome gradually as each rider broadens their personal experience with many different horses. In this way the commonly used words and concepts gradually flame into vivid colours of understanding – a knowledge which can only exist in the act of doing.

004 An Elaboration of Practical Mental Attitudes

1) Our riding will always radiate beauty and joyfulness when we are motivated by respect and love for the horse. This outlook, above all, helps us to overcome the inevitable difficulties encountered on the way to discovering the horse.

2) If we are to raise ourselves up to higher levels of equestrian expression, we need to become constructively self-critical and develop a refined degree of self-control. An essential part of this lies in striving to put aside our ego. The earthy ego ever threatens to warp our ability to assess ourselves and our performance objectively. Only when our desire to learn is constantly tempered by modesty and a genuine interest in the horse's well-being, will we be on the path which leads to the blossoming of true horsemanship.

3) Essentially, the 'living moment' of our own practice is the only truth that exists. Each rider must travel every inch of the road personally – no one else can do it for us. Nonetheless, theoretical study and taking lessons are vital directional aids,

much like having a road map and a personal guide, which can help us on our way to finding constructive purpose and joyfulness in our relationship with the horse.

4) Through our instructor as mediator we need to learn how to read the horse's body language. This is the key to gaining understanding of its physical and psychological nature, and constitutes the chief guideline through which we can come to know how to influence the creature suitably. If we develop our 'feel' and let the horse be our guide from moment to moment, we will be less prone to follow unproductive ways, or be needlessly diverted by baseless theoretical preconceptions.

5) It is entirely the duty of each rider to work diligently if high equestrian standards are to be attained. No matter how good the instructor or horses may be, unless we are eager, open-minded and receptive, only mediocre results can be expected.

6) The horse is in no way interested in our personal ambitions. Only when we have the correct combination of appropriate physical and mental attitudes, and have developed an adequately clear administration of our aids, will the horse readily comply.

7) Horses are a far greater *constant* than is commonly believed. Variations in the quality of their performance are most often produced by fluctuations in the rider's own physical or mental state. It can be observed, time and time again, that when the rider is in a good mood and is feeling well, the horse will usually go well. Conversely, when the rider in a poor mood, is burdened with worries, or lacks emotional control, the horse usually goes badly. Invariably, horses accurately mirror our favourable as well as undesirable attributes (031, 068, 070).

8) It is the rider's complete and sole responsibility, being the more intelligent partner, to find logical solutions to all problems. There are always reasons … never excuses.

9) There is only one kind of mistake, that is, the *fundamental* mistake. Regardless of how advanced the exercise, if the performance is defective, one can directly trace that fault to a lack in the fundamental training of either the horse or the rider.

10) We must learn to distinguish between a judicious, kind leadership, needed to guide the horse with firmness, persistence

and clarity, and an arrogant dictatorship which is enforced through thoughtless subjugation of the animal. The former encourages the horse's willing participation; the latter only pilfers, forces and violates, and can never lead to harmonious beauty.

11) We must come to recognize our own limitations in order to avoid the mistake of demanding work from the horse which we ourselves are incapable of controlling. From this realistic state of self-acceptance we will be able to grow progressively and consistently, and gain genuine enjoyment from small daily successes.

12) It is far too seldom appreciated what a huge task dressage riding is. Therefore we so frequently see riders over-facing their horses and themselves, and consequently having to resort to force, home-baked aids and trickery, in order to produce *supposed* results. Grade-schoolers do not learn basic mathematics by incessantly repeating university-level calculus problems. Yet precisely such concepts are used in the training of both horses and riders. Clearly, unless there is a solid basis, built on a 'step-by-step' understanding of the work being requested, only frustration in the rider and anguish and lameness in the horse can result.

13) Contrary to popular belief, horses do not get bored with simple basic work. If the rider has clear goals in mind, and pays close attention to detail and quality, neither horse nor rider will have time to get bored by even the most rudimentary work – instead, a true sense of accomplishment will be attained. Nothing is more important, more challenging, or more difficult, than cultivating correct basics.

14) A subtle and insidious problem, and a point of some confusion, is that the horse will readily conform to almost any riding method, provided the demands are relatively consistent. In other words, the horse will also yield to methods that do not regard its nature. This compliance occurs because the creature will do whatever is wanted to escape the wrath of man (should it disobey). Unfortunately, however, false methods usually take their toll on the good creature – either through psychological

trauma, or because its life under saddle is truncated by lameness caused by the unnatural, inefficient mode of locomotion which it has been forced to assume.

15) To work correctly entails dealing with an extremely delicate balance of natural values that can all too easily be ignored or overruled. We should therefore guard against stepping beyond the brink at which we become our own authority, no longer listening to the horse for verification of the quality of our influences. Such a breach readily leads to the imposition of immodest demands at the expense of the horse's health and the correctness of the work. This danger becomes *more* prevalent as we become more advanced.

16) No one can learn without making mistakes. We all have to learn at some time; there is no shame in that. Also, worthwhile things are seldom learned without experiencing some hardship. Suffering on both the horse's and rider's part is noble when the mistakes are honest, and a continuous attempt is made to improve — especially on one's virtues of patience and self-control. If we are conscientious, beautiful roses can grow from the manure of our recognized and corrected mistakes.

17) Our own learning is often acquired at considerable expense to the horses; they experience many contradictions before we have mastered the correct administration and coordination of our aids. All of this the horses generally endure with saintly patience and good humour. Surely then, understanding and empathy for the creatures should always rule, despite our own frustrations and tribulations.

18) Understanding is the key to meaningful practice. We can only become effective critics of our own work once we begin to know what the necessary criteria are. Many years of study are required, under close guidance, to learn to recognize all the fine nuances which differentiate the *nature-friendly*, 'Classical' form of riding from trick, artificial, or forced methods. Besides studying the work of the Masters, much can be learned from observing others ride, provided we remain objective in our criticism (have a truly studious attitude), and empathize with the person we are watching (walk a mile in another's shoes).

19) A close rapport, based on respect, is the backbone of good horsemanship. We must respect the horse's physical strength and, with the utmost of care, regard its nature. The horse's role is to learn to respect its intellectually superior rider, and to give itself willingly to the guidance. However, we must *earn* this respect through fair, consistent handling, and by discreetly utilizing praise and correction to help the horse understand our wishes.

20) Since the horse's reactions are many times faster than man's, it is only through conditioning with consistent work, and through our ability to prepare both ourselves and the horse with *timely* aiding, that an element of predictability – the nucleus of a smooth performance – is established.

21) If the horse becomes frightened and shies, or when it has been suddenly startled, our attitudes and reactions should be those which will help maintain the horse's confidence in us. It would be a mistake to pull the horse about angrily, because this would only confirm in the horse's mind that there was truly something to be frightened of. Instead, we should ignore that which is exciting or frightening the horse and, with a nonchalant air, urge the horse to continue with the task at hand (if necessary using a reassuring voice). The rider must learn to become a strong, reliable and just leader … a kind, firm guiding force (070, 071, 072).

22) Punishment

    (a) When should one resort to punishment?

        Generally, punishment should be an *extreme rarity*. In most instances we should think in terms of *correction* instead. Considerable experience and understanding are required to determine whether punishment[2] is actually warranted. The following points should certainly be taken into account:

        Am I physically stiff, or mentally tight, irritable, angry, nervous, or afraid?

        Were my aids correct and clear?

        Is the horse capable of executing the work requested or am I over-facing it?

---

[2] As opposed to just using a clearer, more assertive aid.

During grooming, saddling up, or handling from the ground, did my own actions, insensitivity or carelessness[3] startle the horse, or cause it to kick, or bite?

(b) How can we punish fairly?

If we determine that the horse must be punished, it should be done quickly and methodically, not out of ill-temper or lack of self-control − venting our frustrations on the animal. We do best when we are emotionally detached. We should think in terms of a clearer, more emphatic aid to underscore our intent, and to convince the horse that we mean business. Usually one smart whack with the stick, or an emphatic aid with the spur is more than adequate. Under certain circumstances, a stern voice aid can suffice to re-establish our authority. If the horse is not corrected immediately the misdemeanour is committed, it will not understand why it was punished.

(c) How much punishment is necessary?

The type and amount of punishment should be carefully suited to the character and sensitivity of the horse, and be proportionate to the severity of the infraction. *To be effective, any and all punishment/correction should be* **extremely** *brief*, it should, literally, not last for more than a second.

(d) The *come back*. (What to do after the correction has been made).

This last stage is essential to success but it is often neglected: reaffirming continued friendship and confidence. Once the correction has been made, do not linger on the matter: proceed immediately with a fresh start, as though nothing had happened, and reward the horse for even the slightest signs of cooperation. In this way the horse will readily learn that compliance with the rider's requests is rewarded with kindness, encouragement and praise, but that disobedience is met with unpleasant reactions. Bear no grudges. Correct … forgive … forget … move on …!

---

[3] For example: tighten the girth gently and only gradually. Similar care must be taken while grooming − the horse is not a carpet!

Note: Riders today seem to have become blunted to the concept of people roughing-up their horses and have come to consider this to be a necessary, even normal, part of working and training. For the knowledgeable horseman, however, it is a fail-safe sign that, if horses need to be ridden strongly and roughly, or frequently need to be 'beaten the heck out of' before they apparently submit and 'go well(?!)', then the training is of the poorest order.

23) Ideal harmony is a product of trust. It cannot be dictated or forced out of any horse. Rather, it must be willed to come about by each participant, and can only be won by adequate, patient preparation and goodwill towards our four-legged partner.

24) To adequately discharge our role as leader of the equestrian partnership, we must always work with a clear purpose in mind. The following three elements encompass that leadership: regardless of level we must choose and determine
    (a) **the gait**, and a specific length of stride
    (b) accurate **school figures**, with attention to their size and location
    (c) meaningful **exercises**.
    Aimless riding teaches neither us nor the horse anything.

25) It is most productive to end our work with an exercise that the horse can do easily. To finish on a happy note eases the task of training, and helps to prevent the carry-over of negative attitudes, or the souring of the horse for future work.

26) In order to complete the mosaic of horsemanship, it is important that the background scene is conducive to safety, comfort and peace of mind of the horses. Rough, indifferent handling causes the horses to be come distrustful and frightened, or can make them into unpredictable rogues that acquire the obnoxious habits of biting or kicking. Only if they are cared for with conscientious, quiet work and thoughtful handling while feeding, grooming, mucking-out, and in the general cleaning of the stables, will the horses settle down and be in a good frame of mind, and therefore be well prepared for their work in the manège.

Reflections I

— Armed with theory, practice becomes meaningful … through practice, theory is fulfilled.
— Where 'forwardness' is the *physical* matrix, 'right attitude' (of our heart) is the *spiritual* matrix of horsemanship.
— Does the musician *work* the violin? Of course not! We too should endeavour to '*play*' the horse.
— To achieve 'playful ease' we need to learn how to encourage the willing cooperation of the horse.
— A sizeable portion of the riding task lies in coming to grips with oneself.
— Every master has his horse.
— Rider's tact and feel cannot be taught … it is for each of us to develop these within ourselves.
— Dressage is the fundamental obedience training … for the rider!
— As we come to a deeper understanding of the horse's psyche, we discover more and more how dependent we are on the creature's generosity.
— We should be particularly respectful of school horses. Though they are often common creatures, it is upon their patient backs that we are lead to higher levels of horsemanship.
— There is always much to be learned from *each and every* horse. The learning is never done.
— Horses are not bent on 'doing us in': we can only 'do ourselves in' because of poor attitudes, or inexperience.
— Riding has to do with the nature of the horse, not with our whimsical preconceptions or pet theories.
— All that glitters is not Classical riding.
— The line between very right and very wrong can be disconcertingly thin!
— For the true horseman no equestrian task is too menial.
— The challenge of dressage is not necessarily in having the best-moving horse, but to help every horse we ride to move as well as it possibly can.

— 'Submission' is the aim of the dictator. 'Willing participation' is the aspiration of the thoughtful leader ... the true horseman.

— 'I'm trying' is a self-defeating concept. Instead, say 'I'll do my best' (and mean it!).

— If we think of the horse as an adversary, then indeed, it will be so ...

— The horse reads our heart (our innermost feelings, desires, intentions) more than our actions.

— Our most reliable guide? ... Listen to, and trust, our heart and our horse.

— Patience ...

Meteorite. Working trot.

CHAPTER II

The Seat and Position

*Practice the fugue constantly, tenaciously, until you are tired of the subject
and until your hand is so firm and so sure that you can bend the notes to
your will … let us look back to the past: it will be a step forward.*
Guiseppe Verdi

Essence

A correct seat is:
> balanced • harmonious • independent • stretched
> • elastic • poised

Concepts

— The seat … is 'the conductor of the orchestra'.[1]
— The seat is like the potter's hands, it forms and directs the energy.
— The position … a living *statement* of our desire to the horse.
— Settling down; like pouring sand, each grain finds its place.
— Direct the energy, let the horse *move* itself.
— Upper body … like an ostrich feather – it has a spine, but is soft around the edges.
— Antidote to stiffness … movement … 'boogie' with the horse.
— Long, open front line … our commitment to forwardness.
— Hip joints … loose … always loose.
— Seat bones/saddle … no gaps.
— To centre our body … puppet hanging from a string.

[1] Egon von Neindorff.

13

005 Introduction: The Physical Attitudes

Within the physical attitudes we encompass the modes of the rider's seat and position. When considering the suitability of riders' basic 'raw materials' for the equestrian task, the physical attributes are secondary to the mental ones.[2] Even though it may take many years of diligent work to gain independence and control of individual body parts, most physical problems, outside of major bodily incapacitation, can be dealt with and somehow compensated for.

The position must, above all, be a living, practical instrument and, though correctness is of great importance, we must not lose sight of the overriding need to remain thoroughly supple within this correctness. Involuntary tensions in the rider hamper the clarity and influence of the aids, and restrict the freedom of movement in the horse's back, adversely affecting the forwardness and purity of the gaits. The good position and seat should have an athletic poise, or bearing; a physical tone completely free from stiffness or contortion. This allows energy to flow freely through both the rider's and horse's body.

Despite this acknowledgment, it is important to realize and accept that an excellent seat and position is, with few exceptions, the fruit of hard work. Only after many years of persistent effort in stretching stubborn, unwilling tendons and muscles of the hip joints and thighs, and correcting sloppy habits, such as slouched shoulders and collapsed front lines, will the rider ultimately have produced a riding instrument that can carry out the task of influencing the horse both correctly and effortlessly.

It is quite clear that during the initial years of 'forming' the seat and position, the rider may occasionally be a bit cramped and uncomfortable, and that consequently the horses will temporarily not go very well. That is a price we should, nevertheless, be willing to pay, realizing that as it becomes easier to maintain a suitable posture, ease and natural suppleness will gradually rule once more. To quote the words of Richard Wätjen, 'A fundamentally incorrect seat and position cannot be corrected

[2] Poor mental attitudes are most destructive, and not much of real value can be produced until the rider's mentality, outlook, or philosophy has improved. This is so even if the rider enjoys good health, and perfect physical conformation for riding.

through softness [ease]'.[3] This certainly does not mean that the beginner cannot experience some good, relaxed moments. Yet, if we look only for ease and comfort before we have trained our bodies, nothing but mediocrity and compromise can result.

It cannot be sufficiently strongly recommended to get this 'body forming' phase over with as early as possible. Longeing is of great help *if* done under the eye of an experienced instructor. Do stretching exercises off the horse daily, and make good posture a continual habit, *all day long*, not just during riding! Furthermore, even once a correct seat and position have been achieved, it should be realized that fairly constant, daily attention should be spent on maintenance to prevent regression. In this respect, the rider's posture is not unlike a house or garden which can quickly fall into disrepair without regular care.

006 Five Major Position Corrections[4]

— Head up
— Stomach forward[5]
— Hands vertical
— Knees closed[6]
— Heels down

The position corrections must be kept in as simple a form as possible, so that they are easily remembered during practice sessions. Simplicity of the workload, that is, staying with one theme, is an important key to acquiring any new physical attribute.

If, after having taken instruction, a rider has other corrections to make which pertain specifically to him/herself, then these should be added, in simple form, to the five given above. No seat or position will improve without the frequent mental repetition of these points, followed by the immediate physical correction.

[3] From Richard Wätjen's book, *Dressage Riding*, J. A. Allen & Co.
[4] Egon von Neindorff.
[5] Solar plexus and navel leading. Raise the solar plexus. Long front line. While making this correction take care not to hollow the lower back. The rider's spine should form an elongated 'S' shape when seen from the side. There is such a thing as too hollow, and too round.
[6] Needing to have the knees 'closed' is a gentle concept, and should not be translated into clamping-on or unnecessary gripping.

007 The Seat

The seat is composed of two major parts: 50 per cent is formed by the rider, the other 50 per cent is made up by the horse. However, both of these equal portions are entirely the responsibility of the rider. The rider is both the chicken and the egg! In other words, we must become fully conversant with bringing our own bodies into a suitable attitude;[7] *and* we must become competent in knowing how to help the horse to go correctly under us – so that it 'completes' the seat. Unless we are capable of causing our horse to carry us on an elastic back, originating from engaged hindquarters, a good seat cannot be cultivated. Only such combined correctness of our seat and position, elastically balanced upon the supple, forward, balanced motion of the horse, can consummate a true unity. Clearly, in order to cultivate a good seat, we must acquire a very thorough knowledge of the workings of the whole horse.

The rider's hips and seat, the thigh down to the knee, and the hand and forearm to the elbow, must become part of the horse entirely. The only physical parts of the rider which remain the rider's own are the head and upper body, the arm from shoulder to elbow, and the lower legs. The supple controlling links between these categories are:

The lower back, the lumbar vertebrae, acting as the chief controlling factor through which all aids are transferred to the horse.

The supple shoulders/elbows, which act as buffers to the horse's mouth.

The relaxed hip joint, knee and ankle joint which, most importantly, allow the seat bones to settle unrestrictedly and evenly on the saddle, and also give the lower leg the ability to aid independently.

008 Correct Position and Attitude of the Seat[8]

With the head held upright, a vertical body, and a long, open front line, we should attend to the following points.

---

[7] Irrespective of how well or poorly the horse is going!

[8] **Note:** Being ever interactive and interdependent, no part of our anatomy relating to the seat and position and its influences on the horse is ever wholly separate from any other, nevertheless, for the sake of analysis, each single element will be scrutinized individually.

1) **We must *let* our weight *rest*, straight down into the deepest part of the saddle**. This is the very foundation, the indispensable principle, on which our entire aiding system must be built.

2) **Rest on the two seat bones and on the pubic bone**. These *three* points, forming a **'triangle'**, must be as though welded onto the saddle at all times.[9]

3) **Hips leading.** The whole hip should have the *attitude* of being held ahead of us, steadily into the front of the saddle, with greater or lesser forward pressure as needed.[10] This is inseparable from the concept of letting the 'front line' *draw* the whole 'triangle' forward into the front of the saddle. 'Hips leading' (with forward-*urging* energy coming from the top of the hips, where our belt crosses our spine), and 'front line leading' (with forward-*drawing* energy coming from the navel/solar plexus area), should be seen as synonymous concepts, an equal value of 'forward desire' deriving from both of these elements *simultaneously*.

   'Pelvic Tilt'[11] is an essential aspect of 'hips leading'. Through its subtle attitude adjustments we can determine *from which part of our 'triangle'* the forward-urging/drawing is more emphasized; more from the back of the seat bones, or more from the crotch (021).

4) **Equal weight on *both* seat bones**, except when introducing the bend, *initiating* circles and changes of rein, curved lines, two-track work, or when cantering on, in which case the inside seat bone should *momentarily* have a little more weight in it (021, 032: 1).

5) **Sit centrally and squarely in the saddle**. Do not collapse onto one hip.[12]

---

[9] No 'gaps' between the seat bones/pubic bone and saddle.

[10] Hips leading is only an attitude, which generates an increased forward-urging 'energy pattern' as needed. Regardless of how much we emphasize this attitude we must not lean back with the upper body; nor should the lower back be hollowed. It is also not to be an active 'pumping', or pushing or shoving at each stride … it is a steady forward-urging attitude of the seat. Furthermore, hips leading is an aiding influence, and can therefore be given with greater or lesser intensity, see 022.

[11] 'Pelvic tilt' must be achieved, (a) without raising the pubic bone off the saddle, (b) without collapsing the front line, and (c) without leaning backward! For further details see 021, 022, and 060; and x-ray photos, page 41.

[12] To help us feel central and even down both halves of our body, we can think of being suspended by a string from the middle of the head.

6) **Hips parallel to the horse's hips.** While riding on curved lines, or while bending the horse, the rider's inside hip should be held more emphatically forward.[13]
7) **Hip joints totally loose at all times.** Imagine that there are no muscles or tendons attached to the hip joints whatsoever, only bones rattling around loosely ... turn the hips to water.
8) **The buttock muscles must be relaxed and opened.** This is in conjunction with relaxed thighs and legs which hang naturally. Think of stretching the seat bones wide across the saddle like cling wrap (021, 022).

009 Upper Body and Shoulders

— **Upper body must be open, stretched, free and independent** at all times.
— **Long, open front line.** The rider's front line begins under the chin, and ends at the crotch. It should be made as long as possible by raising the solar plexus *gently* up-and-back into the collar. This is part and parcel of 'drawing the chin into the collar', that is, filling the nape of the neck (014). Avoid becoming 'chesty' through puffing the chest up under the chin; the top of the chest, just below the collar-bones, should remain fairly flat (see summary at end of 009).

The upper body should make a capital 'D', when looked at from the side.[14] Or imagine the spine to be straight and tall like a ship's mast, and that the front line is a billowing sail being filled by a breeze from behind.[15] *Without our hollowing the lower back*, this

---

[13] This should **not** be achieved by letting the outside seat bone empty out or lag behind. Both seat bones must be forward with the horse's movements, but the inside one is emphasized yet a bit more; this could be either a more downward and/or more forward pressure, as needed.

[14] If the front line is collapsed, and the shoulders are rounded, the body forms an ineffective capital 'C'.

[15] The sail may not 'luff'. There must be an even forward pressure at all points along the front line; no part should be even slightly emptier of this 'forward-drawing' quality. Common faults are dropping the solar plexus into the tail bone, or pulling the stomach backwards at the belt line. They are false concepts of what 'driving from the seat/position' means.

billowing sail helps to *draw* the whole seat and position steadily forward into the front of the saddle (solar plexus/navel always leading the way).[16]

— **Shoulders back and down.** *A stretched, open front line with raised solar plexus is an indispensable prerequisite to achieving a correct, natural, relaxed, 'hanging' shoulder position.* The observer should see only the back of the rider's upper arm when looking at the rider from the side. If either the shoulder-blades or the rider's back are bulging out from behind the upper arm, the ideal has not yet been achieved.

Note: A helpful exercise to find the correct shoulder position is to make an 'upside-down U'[17]: move the shoulders all the way (a) forward and down, (b) forward and up, (c) up and back, (d) back and down.[18] When the corrections have been well made, the 'points' of the shoulders should end up pointing *very slightly* backward. Also, one should be able to see the front of the armpits when looking at the rider from the side.

— **Shoulders level.** When looking at the rider from the front or back, the shoulders must be at the same height. To help achieve this evenness of the body and shoulders, think of being a puppet hanging from a string by the top of the head.
— **Shoulders parallel to the horse's shoulders.** To achieve this requirement, while we are bending the horse or riding on curved lines, we must turn our whole upper body *inward* from the waist. Furthermore, without in any way altering the weight in the outside rein, the whole outside of our

---

[16] This helps us get away from all the senseless, unproductive shoving and pushing forward of the horse with the seat, and assists us to be truly **with** the movement. The seat can and should assist the horse to go forward, but that is an *attitude*, not a huge physical shoving.

[17] Concept in quotes, Monty Smith.

[18] These points should be exaggerated until the correct position becomes easier to maintain – more natural.

19

body, including the hip, must always be well *'brought along with'* the horse's movement. To avoid lagging behind with the outside seat bone/hip/thigh, think of 'turning a piano stool'.[19]

Note: It is easy to visualize the appropriate amount of turning our body needs if we imagine **three windows**. They are tall and narrow, each one only a foot wide, but reaching from the ceiling to the floor. The centre window is directly over the horse's head; the left one is just left of the horse's left ear; the right one just right of the horse's right ear. When going straight, right or left, we should point our vision *and the energy of our entire body* through the corresponding window.

Front Line summary

The front line is an indispensable basis, a core element, of the effective seat and position. *The front line empowers the seat.*

The front line is made up of three essential and inseparable elements:

(a) Raise the solar plexus – stretch from under the chin to the crotch.
(b) Shoulders back and down.
(c) Bent, pointy, and 'heavy' elbows.

By assuring that the hand is always on the line from the bit to the elbow, and by thinking of the elbows as being elastically anchored in the middle of the spine, these correct front line attitudes enable the energy (which the horse brings to the bit because of its forward desire) to be transferred directly to the horse's back via the seat bones. These are the root elements which make 'completion of the circuit' possible (041).

---

[19] Concept in quotes, Susan Terrall. (Those who are experienced in 'raising a glass or two' can think of turning a bar stool).

010 Thigh and Knee

Only once we are properly settled on our seat (see 008), is it productive to attend to the leg/thigh position. *It is not possible to position the leg/thigh correctly without an absolutely loose, relaxed hip joint.* In fact, the relaxed hip joint is totally indispensable to achieving a correct, effective, and harmonious seat. Leg corrections must not be forced. The main points are:

— Open the hip joint *outward* as wide as possible.
— Turn the lower leg *inward* (until feet are parallel to the horse's sides).
— Lay the whole leg relaxed on the horse's sides.[20]

These corrections give the horse's body plenty of space between the thighs, and the knees will still be able to come in contact with the saddle as they should: snuggle the knee *gently* into the saddle flap. The legs should simply 'hang' down, like two sopping-wet towels. They gain the necessary substance, so that they do not dangle sloppily, by being stretched down elastically through the heels.[21] The thigh muscle must lie relaxed on the saddle. If tension is detected anywhere in the hip joint or leg, we can overcome this by 'fluffing' the leg up a bit, like a pillow, and then laying it on the horse again. Or we can use the old longeing exercise, 'scissoring' the legs, until we feel better 'let down' on the seat bones – useful at the walk and trot (rising!![22] or sitting).

The *energy pattern* of the upper leg, from the hip joint to the knee, should point to the ground; imagine a kneeling attitude.[23] The leg should not be so straight, however, that we begin to sit on our thighs (fork or crotch seat). Conversely, if the knees are too high, we cannot

---

[20] It can be helpful to draw the thigh muscle out from underneath the femur by hand.
[21] This is not to be forced, we should avoid jamming the heels down.
[22] Though this exercise is commonly used during longeing, there are clear advantages to using it during normal riding, even at the rising trot, especially for riders who suffer from stiffness or tensions. This was brought to my attention by Susan Terrall. Good exercise!
[23] Or, *without in any way actually pulling the leg back physically*, think of leaving the legs on the road behind you, as you travel on without them. Or, think of sitting ahead of, or beyond the legs. These are only mental concepts, not facts. They are meant to help us to get the correct *essences* or attitudes, the correct '*flow of energy*' through our bodies.

effectively bring our weight into the seat bones and through to the ground (chair seat).

011 Lower Leg and Foot

— **Lower legs must hang vertically**, when looking at the rider from the front or back.

— **Heels must be on the vertical line** running through the centre of the rider's shoulder and hip, when observing the rider from the side.[24] The leg aids are more effectively given from this position, and the rider is better able to find independent balance.

— **Lower legs must be well turned inward**[25] from the knee down, until the foot is almost parallel to the horse's sides. This turning of the lower legs is done wholly in conjunction with opening the hip joints outward. Though it is affected by it, *the thigh should not be **actively** involved in this inward turning*. We should give the leg aids with the inside of the calves, usually with only the top 4–6 inches (10–15 cm). Also, imagine giving the aids with the shins. This helps prevent the following unproductive attitudes:
  – sitting on the back of the thighs
  – drawing up the legs during aiding
  – clamping-on with the lower leg
  – digging at the horse with the heels.

— **Heels must be the lowest point of the rider**.[26] This is an *end result* of sitting correctly, when the whole leg ends up hanging relaxed in the stirrup. *The heels should say the same things as the seat bones say.* Keep the ankle joint relaxed. This:
  – gives our whole seat/position an attitude of going forward with the horse

[24] This placement should not be forced. As the rider's weight settles better into the saddle, this requirement will be achieved in a relaxed, natural way, as it should.

[25] This is best achieved by thinking 'heel out, *then* leg on', instead of just pulling the toe inward, which tends to cause residual tensions in the hip/thigh and leg.

[26] The drawn-up heel has a restraining, withholding effect on the horse's forward energy; it is an inharmonious attitude.

– is the root of stretching from heel to head
– helps draw the weight into the seat
– helps to stabilize the lower leg.
— **Lower leg in constant contact** on the horse's sides, with a light, elastic, caressing quality. The leg must 'breathe' with the horse. It should be as quiet as possible, though it may move slightly with the motion of the horse's body. An exaggerated, incessant tapping is usually a sign of tension.

012 Arms, Elbows and Wrists

The upper arms should hang down vertically from relaxed, drawn back shoulders[27] and lie lightly by the rider's sides. *The elbow is the conversion point of the energy; it should always be relaxed, bent, pointy, and heavy.* This essential function and attitude of the elbow is achieved by raising the forearm until the hand is on a straight line from the bit to the elbow. Let the forearm be relaxed[28] (boneless chicken) and simply become a part of the rein leather (the reins start at the elbows!). The shoulders, elbows, wrists, and fingers should always be supple and elastic. The wrist may not be broken inward or outward, nor upward or downward. The back of the hand and the forearm should form a smooth, continuous line. Mistakes to watch out for:
— Stiff downstretched or outstretched arms (not enough bend in the elbow).
— 'Broken' wrists (either rounded or hollowed, or broken up or down).
— Hands which are boring downward (trying to get, or keep, the horse's head down).
— Hands held too high (as if reading a newspaper).
— Any stiffness in the shoulder, elbow, forearm, wrist, hand or fingers

[27] This is easier to achieve without tension when the front line is well stretched and solar plexus raised, see 009.
[28] Even when raised to the correct height, the forearm should have a relaxed 'heavy-ish' or 'leaden' quality, and not the sort of light 'uppity' attitude one would use to toss a salad. When we have an open front line in conjunction with such forearm attitudes, it allows the energy from the reins to arrive unimpeded in the seat bones, and vice versa.

013 Hands

Both hands should be held at the same height. They must be held vertically, thumbs uppermost, and with the little fingers slightly closer together than the thumbs. This is an important requirement, for it has been well established that, with this position, the hand is at its most sensitive and articulate, and it facilitates the best, most direct contact between the bit and the seat bones. The hand must be perfectly quiet in relation to the horse's mouth. From this comes the old saying, 'The hand stands still, but moves anyway'.[29] The attitude of the hands should always be alive, that is, ever-relevant to the living moment. This does not mean that they should actively fiddle about, but rather that they must be elastic and feeling; not stark, hard or unfriendly.

We must avoid having the knuckles pointing to the ground. Instead, the little fingers should generally point towards the horse's mouth with a giving attitude. The fingers should be relaxed.

014 Head Position

The head must be held upright, since only in this mode can the weight of the entire upper body fall correctly into the seat. The head should be carried with a noble bearing – think of carrying a book on your head. A hanging head nullifies the driving ability of the seat, as does the nodding head; these attitudes lessen the effectiveness of all weight aids. In general, looking down also greatly reduces the rider's ability to feel the horse working under the saddle – so '*look to the horizon*'.[30] Have the back of the head stretched up and forward to the sky, so that the eyebrows 'shade' your vision (like a peaked cap).[31] This attitude 'fills' the nape of the neck, and helps draw the whole spine into a useful, consolidated, poised unit.[32] Raising the solar plexus, and drawing the chin *gently*

[29] Egon von Neindorff.
[30] Concept in quotes, Michael Gutowski.
[31] This is closely associated with the action of raising the solar plexus up and back into the collar.
32 This applies especially to the lower back, the lumbar vertebrae.

into the back of the collar are also components of this correction. To stick the chin out (vulture attitude!) lessens the effectiveness of the seat.

By and large, one's vision should be directed over the horse's head. Avoid tipping the top of the head inward or outward, especially during work on curved lines.

015 Putting it all Together

This is a brief synopsis, in logical sequence, for making seat and position corrections:

—   *Let* the weight *rest* straight down in the deepest part of the saddle.[33]
—   Rest on the 'triangle'.
—   Stretch from heel to head (the more we stretch, the softer we should be).
—   'Carry a book on your head' (fill nape of neck; look to horizon).
—   Now open the front line[34] and *draw* the 'triangle' forward in the saddle with it; navel and solar plexus leading the way.
—   Then, 'hips leading', as needed; and adjust 'pelvic tilt' attitude, as needed.[35]
—   Let legs hang from *loose* hip joints; snuggle knees *gently* into saddle flaps.
—   *Think* of kneeling; or dropping the legs off, leaving them on the road behind you, and going on without them. (Do not force this, just think of it, and let it happen.)

---

[33] Regardless of which other corrections we make this first requirement must always be maintained. It is the foundation.

[34] This always has three elements: raise the solar plexus; shoulders back and down; bent, 'pointy', heavy elbows.

[35] The more the hips lead, the more the front line should lead. The front line empowers the seat (See 008: 3).

— Ride your hips *and the horse's body* through your elbows.

— Ride your front line (body) through your shoulders.

016 Criteria for Correct Rising Trot

— We have a mobile, dynamic centre of balance which moves between the foot and the knee.

— We must have a well-stretched position, and freedom and independent balance of the upper body.

— The inclination of the upper body should be *slightly* tilted forward;[36] the angle is directly related to the centre of balance of the horse. If the horse is tense and rushing on the forehand, the upper body should be brought forward slightly to coincide with the horse's centre of balance; only then can the horse's rhythm and balance be restored through either half-halting or driving. Once the horse is in balance, and allows itself to be driven, then the upper body can come somewhat closer to the vertical again.

— The horse should move the rider (a trampoline effect); it shouldn't be necessary to stand up forcibly.

— The motion of the seat should be forward and back, the hips moving through the elbows; as opposed to an exaggerated up and down, jack-in-the-box attitude. The rise should be as small as possible.

— The lower back should be steady, neither hollow while rising, nor round while sitting. The correct steadiness of the spine[37] can best be achieved when the hip joints are truly relaxed and loose.

— Rise as the horse's outside front leg goes forward and, in order to exercise both sides of the horse equally, remember

---

[36] Unlike at the walk, sitting trot and canter, when the body should be absolutely vertical. The correct angle is determined by the rider finding open, free, independent balance with the upper body.

[37] Where the rider's torso, made up of the body and hip, remains as a unit. The wobbly, loose, 'doughy' lower back is to be avoided.

the need to switch diagonals when changing the rein.[38]
Sitting as the inside hind leg bears weight also assist in
animating the horse.

— Be well relaxed and 'let down' – sit and rise honestly. A non-
sitting, hovering over the saddle is ineffective. However, do
not drop harshly onto the horse's back when sitting.

— Care must be taken to rise and sit squarely, to avoid a
twisting or mincing motion of either the hips or the
shoulders.

— The knee and lower leg must be steady. The knee acts as a
pivot.

— The weight should go clearly into the relaxed ankles at each
stride, the heels showing a slight dip each time the rider
rises.

— Relative to the horse's mouth, the hands are to be *absolutely
motionless*, without exception! This, however, does not mean
rigid.

A Few Words About Saddles and Riding Breeches

The use of friction materials, such as suede-covered breeches or
saddles, does not actually help the rider to find the *real* depth of seat
required to achieve Classical standards. Quite contrary, in fact – such
artificial aids to adhesion give the rider a false sense of closeness.
They actually prevent the correct development of depth and
harmony, which is based on balance and an unrestricted fall-of-
weight into the seat bones, and down through the heels towards the
ground.

Regarding the fit of riding breeches, it appears that those available
today are cut mainly with fashion in mind. Though made of elastic
material, these skin-tight breeches, or 'sausage casings', do not allow
the thigh and buttock muscles to relax and form naturally to the
saddle. It is best to get breeches that have an inch or two of extra

---

[38] During training it can be helpful to change diagonals, back and forth, independent of
changing the rein. This can help to encourage the horse to use both hind legs evenly.

space in the thigh and seat; they should fit lightly and loosely in those areas. This will be found helpful especially for those who are either muscle-bound or who have heavy thighs. Learning to sit properly is a huge enough task that one doesn't need the added burden of being held back by restrictive clothing.

The trend towards saddles with 'deep seats'(!!) is another totally misleading phenomenon. The rider's own seat must be deep; meaning that it is well let down, and has found purest harmony with the horse. It is utter nonsense and self-deception to imagine that, just because the saddle has a high pommel and cantle, the rider will automatically be sitting more deeply. The finest saddles are those which are *neutral*; that is, they *allow* the rider to sit correctly, yet in no way 'put the rider into (any) position'. The true position and seat are a result of years of patient work and *correct* experience.

Reflections II

—   '*The seat is the alpha and the omega of riding*' – Egon von Neindorff.
—   The position is formed by 'carrying', not by 'holding' … and by 'toning', not by 'tensions'.
—   The hands must remain, strictly, each on its own side of the horse's neck.
—   It is a serious fault to be sitting in the back of the saddle, being pushed along by the cantle. Leave plenty of saddle out behind the seat.
—   If the rider's heels are continuously drawn up, the seat is fundamentally incorrect (inhibits the forward motion of the horse).
—   Remember to let the horse do the work; the rider is only the control centre. 'You carry me, I just want to sit here!'
—   The seat cannot be cultivated as an isolated entity – its quality is directly related to the correctness of its influence on the horse.
—   An artificial, superficial position without practical purpose is worthless. A good seat, without a technically correct

position, is impossible.

— It is essential that our breathing remains relaxed, even, and free, especially during aiding.

— The hands are only ever as good as the seat.

— The rider can sit over the horse, on the horse, or *in* the horse. The last of these is the ultimate goal.

— All leg aids should be given from a closed knee, in gentle contact with the saddle flap.

— Too high a hand position robs the horse of the use of its back, and snubs-off the impulsion from the hindquarters.

— Once we have acquired a good seat, we must use the power of its *razor's edge* wisely, and never against the horse. Like the surgeon's scalpel, it can either heal or destroy with ease!

Atlantis. Shortened working canter right.

CHAPTER III

The Aids

GIVE AN AID ● GET A RESPONSE ● STOP GIVING THE AID

Essence

— After each aid – go back to 'zero'.[1]
— Resolve each request before asking for the next.
— Delegate? ... Set the horse up ... leave it alone ... so it goes on its own.
— 'Hot potato aids' ... quick, bright, light – not long, dead, strong.
— Signals, not 'heaving and ho-ing', that get the horse going.
— Hold nothing ... correct – flow ... re-correct – flow ... *hold nothing!*
— Drive a bit – get a response – coast a bit.

Concepts

— Note: the word is 'AID' ... to help! ... we are to encourage the horse ... not force it.
— Aids ... agents, messengers that do the work for us.
— If we're not ready, we shouldn't ask.
— Remain emotionally neutral, detached.

---

[1] Return to neutrality.

— Freedom, independence … a dance, a partnership.
— Stuck, holding … a prison!
— A little air in our joints while aiding – *breathe* the aids into the horse.
— Effectiveness? … As little as possible, as much as necessary.
— 'Goldie Locks' principle? … too strong … too weak – *just right!*
— 'Pay attention', is meaningless … 'Do *this*' (specific request) is irresistible!

Introduction

To gain the fullest possible benefit from the contents of this chapter, it is essential that the reader does not falsely assume that there is a cast-iron method to the administration of aids. Each moment of riding is unique. And so we must learn to use a truly dynamic language, based on *living*, natural principles, when addressing the horse. It will be discovered that, within the basic parameters presented below (*which are indispensable to correct aiding*) there is nevertheless considerable flexibility when applied in practice.

An inherent by-product of analysis is that we need to scrutinize the many facets of aiding one by one. This can create a rather fractured picture. We should therefore avoid isolating the points presented, as much as possible, realizing that only through a harmonious, interactive use of our signalling system, 'The Symphony of Aids', can a competent guidance of the horse evolve.

To acquire suitable habits in any learning procedure implies that, first of all, many new and unfamiliar facets need to be brought into the conscious mind before the desired unconscious, habitual behaviour can be formed. Naturally, the best results cannot be expected during this 'conscious effort' phase. Only once correct habits are firmly established will our performance take on the essential aura of ease.

Though we need to work diligently, trying too hard can bring mental and physical tensions which result in blockage of the learning process. As an antidote to this, if we run into difficulties, it is important to go ahead and JUST RIDE!,[2] with a certain amount of free abandon.[3] This means to work with a happy, positive attitude. We could, for example, pretend we're on a hack for a few minutes until our over-serious or over-critical attitudes have melted away, and the horse will soon feel more relaxed and approachable. With a clear basic goal in mind, we can ride the horse forward on specific school figures, and in the gait of our choice. Then, out of this more realistic and stable set of circumstances, we can gradually introduce any new or more challenging aspects, playfully experimenting with them a few at a time, so as not to become so entangled in theory that we can no longer see the riding for the aids.

017 Definition of the Aids

(a) Aids are signals: the *words* of our riding language – a language of '*feel*'.
(b) Aids must be brief: a *momentary* adjustment of the horse.
(c) Be decisive, *get a response*. Aimless badgering only dulls horses.
(d) When the response comes, *instantly stop* giving the aid; neutralize the hand, leg or seat.[4]
(e) Contrast is the strength and clarity of the aid!

Effective aiding can be summarized by the following 'three-part cycle'. It is one of the core aiding principles on which all our horsemanship can be based:

Give and aid – get a response – stop giving the aid.

---

[2] Think of being a kid on a pony; play confidently with the horse.
[3] This can of course also be taken too far, to the point where we become too careless. As with all things the happy medium is to be sought.
[4] Because the seat is not actually an active aid, but rather influences by its very presence alone, and by subtle attitude changes, we may have a small, passive 'maintaining' attitude; on a scale of 1 to 10, this attitude would be about a '1', or possibly a '2' at most. 10 would represent a very strong driving presence. '0' is used under special circumstances only, see 022.

018 Principles in the Giving of Aids

— **The driving influences (from seat, front line and legs) should predominate**,[5] by far exceeding the receiving or restraining aids of the hands.

— **Work the horse from back to front.** Never pull the horse together by the reins.

— **Use only one *active* aid at any one time**; the other aids remaining passive and supporting.[6]

— **All aids must work in harmony towards one single intention**. No contradictory aids. Keep it simple!

— **Equal weight in both seat bones**; except when giving specific aids, such as bending, changing direction, cantering-on, etc., in which case the inside seat bone is made *momentarily* heavier.

— **Equal pressure in both legs**; except when giving a sideways-yielding aid.

— **Equal pressure in both reins**; except when giving a bending or straightening aid.

Note: The last three points above are goals which we must strive constantly to perfect. They can only be *completed and fulfilled* through gaining the responsiveness of a compliant, supple, balanced horse. As we know, 50 per cent of the seat is made up by the rider, 50 per cent is made up by the horse. The same concept applies to the contact – see 030.

Timing

Split-second, correct timing in giving aids (or praise and correction), and the suitable duration of an aid, are of utmost importance to achieving successful reactions from the horse. If an aid is poorly timed, is too long or short, too weak or strong, it may

---

[5] This does not mean we must drive all the time. It implies that the *forward desire in the horse* is the life-blood of riding; everything else depends on it for success. As soon as the rein influences predominate, horsemanship has departed from our riding.

[6] Do not use an active rein aid without it being well supported in a passive leg, and/or weight aid; a good seat and position 'presence'.

well elicit exactly the opposite effect from that which we had intended.

Listening

The aids should not be a monologue, thundering blindly from the rider. We must learn to listen to the horse, and subject ourselves to its nature, temperament and sensitivity, and to its needs at any given moment – not to mention compensating suitably for the varying external circumstances as they present themselves. Only when we listen very attentively, especially *whilst aiding*, can we give exactly the right amount, and texture, and intonation to each aid; but above all, listening makes it possible for us to hear that ever-critical cue from the horse, indicating *when to stop giving the aid* – the *sine qua non* of effective aiding.

Feeling

An indispensable factor to improved riding lies in cultivating our sensitivity, our 'feel'. *Only when we can feel a result from our aids will the horse begin to react to them consistently.* In other words, it is in the conscious use of an aid, and in the awareness of the reaction it has elicited from the horse, that the difference lies between true aids, and accidental movements on our part.

Needless to say, the quality of the aids is in direct relation to the skill and experience of the rider. The less experienced rider still needs to use relatively coarse, obvious aids. The advanced rider can tune a horse so finely that response is gained from mere suggestions and thoughts.

Delegating

Delegating is the central pillar of good aiding, riding, and training. The technically accurate implementation of the 'three-part cycle' of aid-giving is the key to understanding how to delegate the work to the horse. This bears repeating – *Give an aid. Get a response. Stop giving the aid!* In this way we show the horse what we want, and then we leave it alone, so that we can remain the calm, detached leaders we need to be, while we let the horse do its part of the work.

Through delegating we gain independence, whilst also

optimizing the chances that the creature will offer, from its own initiative and wonderful eagerness, that extra spark of brilliance to the performance. Through such independence we avoid getting tied-up with the horse, lugging on the reins, or having it bulging and leaning against our legs. If such things do happen, we have either not *resolved each and every aid*, and/or we are 'holding' the horse in an attempt to prevent something unwanted from occurring, or from losing something we have gained, neither of which is productive. While we are aiding it can be helpful to think of saying to the horse: 'Come on, *you* do this, I don't want to do it for you. You move your own body!'

Tune the horse with 'hot potato' aids – 'hold' *nothing*. This is the secret to delegating, and remaining gloriously independent.

019 Main Categories of Aids

Basically, there are two main categories of aids: unilateral, and diagonal.

Unilateral aids

The rein, seat bone and leg on the same side act as containing aids. These form the channel through which the horse is guided. They prevent the horse from drifting sideways, and thus keep its energy flowing towards the bit, instead of escaping out the sides. Used *passively*, they are containing aids, the 'river-banks'. Used *actively*, they constitute a corrective aid ('Hey, stay off this leg!), or an overt sideways-yielding aid ('Move over to the wall').[7] (See also section 038, framing the horse.)

Diagonal aids

The inside leg and outside rein, or the outside leg and the inside rein, influence the horse in active and passive diagonal pairs. They are used to affect the bend, or straightness of the horse, or to establish the two-track positions.

A description of these aid applications follows.

---

[7] Usually it is the leg that is active, assisted by a passive 'confirming' of the rein on the same side for leg-yielding (without changing the bend).

020 Basic Functions of the Natural Aiding Tools

The most rudimentary function of the natural riding tools – the seat, hands and legs – is to *passively* contain, form, and guide the horse. Just being in a correct posture, relaxed and well let down on the seat bones (the 'triangle'), makes for this suitable, effective, passive guiding '*presence*'. From this neutral state the basic tools perform specific *main* functions which are given below in **bold** type. The more subtle secondary functions, which may be either active or passive, are given in plain type.

THE ACTIVE DIAGONAL PAIR[8]

INSIDE[9] LEG: gives the **active driving aid**; gives the **active sideways-yielding aid**; secondarily, it acts like a *passive* post around which the horse is bent.[10]

OUTSIDE REIN: **actively controls the pace**, affecting the balance and carriage of the horse (see 060, the half-halt); secondarily, it limits the amount of bend. It is the chief guiding rein.

—   (IF!! it is necessary to be active), the active aid is given by a nudging, pulsing, or vibrating within the application of (aiding) pressure. (Active aids are applied when passive aids do not elicit responses from the horse.)

---

[8] The requirement of only one active aid at any one time still applies. In other words, either the hand may be active, or the leg may be active, but not both at the same time. Furthermore, THESE TOOLS ARE ONLY TO BE ACTIVE WHEN NECESSARY! Once the desired reaction has been achieved from the horse, they should instantly return to their home base of neutrality.

[9] The 'inside' is the side towards which we wish to bend the horse.

[10] The inside leg does **not** bend the horse actively – we bend the horse around it (see 033).

THE PASSIVE DIAGONAL PAIR

OUTSIDE LEG[11]: **passively holds the quarters from swinging out**; as a driving leg, has the same pressure as the inside leg but remains passive (026).

INSIDE REIN: **has no prime function**, other than passively counterbalancing[12] the outside rein to maintain lateral stability, or location of the head/neck. It has only one secondary *active* function: it asks for the flexion or bend,[13] that's all! (see 033).

— The passive aid is constituted by the presence or acceptance of a steady, uniform, living, *elastic* pressure; it does not imply a dead quality.

THE SEAT
All aids must find their base in, or act through the seat to the horse's back (021).

WHAT FUNCTION DOES THE HAND PLAY?
In its function as regulator of the pace, the hand can be compared to the nozzle on the end of a garden hose. When the rider does not take up the contact (loose rein), it would be the same as completely removing the nozzle from the hose; the water, not being restricted, just falls out. When the contact is taken up, the nozzle starts to play

---

[11] When the leg is in the normal position (011) it acts on the horse as a driving aid. If the leg is held back from this position by 4–5 inches (10–13 cm) it acts as a containing aid when passive, and a sideways–yielding aid when used actively and with more pressure.

[12] The hands, via the reins, must continuously, passively, and *interactively* counterbalance one another.

[13] As its only main, active function it obtains the lateral 'flexion' behind the horse's inside ear, jaw. (That is, bending at the tip of the fishing rod, not at its base.) This flexion can only be properly achieved through balanced forwardness of the horse, without which we would merely be breaking the horse up laterally. In the larger picture, the inside rein is part of the 'symphony of aids' which interactively and cooperatively bends the whole horse. Any bending aids must always be well-based in suitable seat/position and leg attitudes. TAKE NOTE: the inside rein only bends the horse, IT MUST NOT BE USED TO 'STEER'.

the role of accurately controlling the amount of water (forward energy) leaving the hose. When the nozzle is shut, the water (horse) stops. When the nozzle opens more or less, and depending on the amount of pressure generated by the pump (driving aids), the result is either a fine, powerful mist (collected work, piaffe), or a strong, forceful jet of water (extended trot).

If there is no pressure control on the pump (ruthless, insensitive use of the driving aids), and should the nozzle be shut (a hard, resisting hand, or tension in the rider), the hose would rupture somewhere along its length (the horse first becomes excited then, if pressure isn't released, the horse would explode by rearing, bucking, or kicking out behind, or becoming evasively crooked, in order to relieve the overload of pressure in its body. The milder manifestations of this would be: tensions, stiffness, resistance, rushing, constrained motion, and choppy gaits).

The nozzle is only of value as a *passive* control when the water pump operates properly. Similarly, the hand only functions correctly in the presence of correct seat and positions attitudes, and when the driving aids, via a responsive horse, supply it with sufficient forward energy.

THE VOICE
Horses react quite readily to the voice. This can be used advantageously, especially during training. When sounds are calm and soothing they have a relaxing, confiding effect. If, however, the voice is stern or sharp, the horse perceives it as a form of chastisement.

THE SPURS AND WHIP
These are considered **artificial aids**, and are only to be used to sharpen the horse's response to the natural aids (074).

021 What is a Weight Aid?

The weight aid is constituted in the ability to determine precisely how and where our centre of balance (weight) falls into our seat bones and pubic bone – the 'triangle'. Gaining mastery over this aspect is central to achieving effectiveness and excellence in our horsemanship. Weight aids are generally subtle, and find their true impact only once we have learned to sit quietly, and cause our centre of balance to coincide with the horse's centre of balance – that is, putting the horse correctly *on the aids* (043, 044). There are two categories of weight aid: unilateral and bilateral.

A unilateral weight aid entails increasing the weight (and/or forward–urging quality) in only *one* of the seat bones.[14] This influences the horse as a bending aid; or a guiding aid; or it can be used during the canter aid; or it can assist us to help the horse to reach better into an 'empty' rein, when the seat bone on that side is more forward–urging (032: 1).

A bilateral weight aid entails the adjustment of weight in *both* seat bones simultaneously and *equally*. This bilateral effect has two elements: (a) thinking of 'hips leading' (008: 3), and (b) is affected by the attitude called '**pelvic tilt**', which enables us to determine precisely from which area of our 'triangle' (made up of the two seat bones and the pubic bone) the increased forward–urging/forward–drawing emphasis comes.

When the influence comes:

(a) more from the back of the seat bones, it has a greater driving effect;
(b) more from the whole 'triangle' evenly, it indicates no particular changes are required from the horse;
(c) more from the crotch, the driving is decreased or entirely suspended; this could be used for young, tense, or sensitive horses, which cannot yet bear stronger driving influences.

'Pelvic tilt' is purely an attitude alteration of the hips. Regardless of which part of our 'triangle' we are emphasizing, *all three points* must remain in contact with the saddle at all times.

---

[14] This does not mean that we should take the other seat bone off the saddle, nor lighten it.

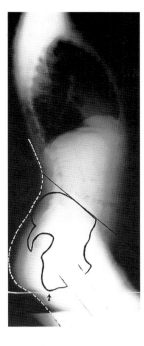

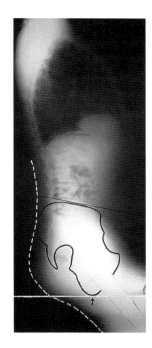

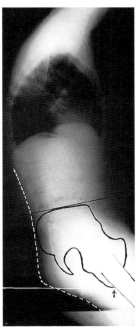

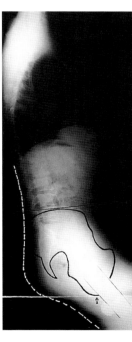

These are actual X-rays of the Author's position, clarifying the various attitudes of the pelvis (outlined in black) and the rider's back (broken white line). The arrow locates the weight-bearing points of the seat bones, which rest on a surface represented by the horizontal white line. The transverse black line shows the angle of the pelvis.

Top left
Hollow back. This fault is often seen with the upper body leaning forward or backward.

Top right
Correct normal seat.

Bottom left
Hunched back. This faulty position is often misconstrued for a driving attitude. The upper body is collapsed, the weight is dissipated and cannot be effectively focused on the seat bones.

Bottom right
Shows an exaggerated example of the pelvic tilt attitude. In practice, there is not actually as much visual difference between this example and the normal seat (above). A photograph cannot adequately demonstrate such a subtle, dynamic attitude adjustment (see 021).

The driving weight aid

The essence of the driving seat is constituted in sitting more deeply *into and with* the motion of the horse; it is a closer 'merging-in-forward-desire-with'. Technically, in conjunction with an emphasized, forward-drawing front line,[15] the hips are held more emphatically forward in the saddle. Yet, *every cell* in our body must partake in this forward desire, and not just the seat bones. If we compare the dynamics of the seat and position to a car, the seat bones or 'triangle' represent only the tyres, 'where the rubber meets the road'. The engine, however, is elsewhere, its forward-urging energy must be generated at the **top** of the pelvis, where our belt crosses over our spine at the back, and/or from the navel in the front (this is to be done without hollowing the lower back!).

Note: any of these 'pelvic tilt' or 'forward-urging' attitudes should **not** be achieved through any hint of backward leaning of the upper body, nor any raising of the pubic bone (crotch) off the saddle, nor any shortening of the front line,[16] nor because of any *active* 'pumping' or 'mincing' in the saddle. Though they have very clear and decisive effects on the horse, these weight influences are explicitly *passive attitudes*. *The optimum seat effect is to be absolutely quiet in relation to the horse's back.*

022 Three Main Attitudes of the Seat

1) **The neutral, 'following' seat** is a relaxed, non-influential, harmonious flowing with the horse's movement (it represents '0' on the influence scale from 0 to 10). It adds nothing to, nor does it detract from, the forward qualities of the gait. If the horse were calm, it would sooner or later coast to a standstill under such a neutral attitude. This attitude could therefore be used during the 'quiet' moments between the aids. This would apply particularly to young horses, or sensitive, nervous, or tense ones, until they

---

[15] The front line **empowers** the seat!
[16] Especially do not draw the stomach back … we must continue to push the stomach well forward, especially during 'pelvic tilt'.

are more accepting of the rider's presence, and thus become more receptive to the driving aids.

2) **The driving or 'maintaining' seat** is achieved through a greater or lesser degree of forward-urging/forward-drawing energy of the seat/position. This is a *'participating'* or *'flowing harmoniously with'* attitude, much as one would have with a dance partner.[17]

   – **In its mild form** ('1' or '2' on the scale) it encourages the horse to maintain the present level of energy.
   – **In a stronger form** (from '2' to '10' on the scale) it would support any request for greater activity from the horse; and could be used during half-halts, transitions, etc. Such increases should be used just temporarily.

Note: Any 'maintaining' or driving attitudes from the seat/position should not degenerate into a visible, active pushing or pumping on the saddle at each and every stride.[18] Instead, they are to be given in a smooth, *steady* manner, *oozing* the horse forward over a number of strides, regardless of the intensity required. Should the horse ignore this steady attitude, then we should use the leg, supported by the stick or spur if necessary, to 'tune' the horse, inciting it to react better to the seat/position attitudes.

3) **'Bracing the back'** is a *brief* alteration in body attitude, emphasizing a more noble, 'carrying' quality of the rider's presence. This has a 'consolidating' effect on the entire torso, especially the lower back and hip. Through this the rein contact is given a clearer 'anchoring point' in the seat bones. It is achieved through accentuating the 'stretch' from heel to head,[19] and broadening the shoulders and the hips while gently breathing in. When used in conjunction with a half-halt on the outside rein (and provided there is adequate forward energy

---

[17] This is difficult to describe. It could be seen as an 'active passivity', or a 'passive activity'. See the **driving weight aid** above.
[18] During any seat attitude alterations, we must not lose the overall quality of letting our weight *rest straight down* into the deepest part of the saddle.
[19] The more we stretch the softer we should be.

present in the horse), it has the effect of causing the horse to gather-up under itself, and thus to find better balance under the rider. The rider's back should not stiffen while bracing, but rather only gain in 'tone', and the hip joints should be 'turned to water' during 'bracing' to assure a good, clear contact between the seat bones and the saddle.

Bracing is a far more subtle influence than is generally appreciated. The observer should hardly be able to see it in the rider, witnessing only its liberating effects on the horse because of improved balance and self-carriage. *This all has to do with softness and finesse, not power!* See 060, half-halt.

023 Points of Optimum Driving Influence from the Seat

1) The **stretch** of the position is emphasized from heel to head. Head held up (carrying a book).
2) A **vertical,** quiet, upper body, with noble bearing. Emphasized, open, front line, drawing the 'triangle' forward in the saddle.
3) **Hips leading,** in conjunction with a suitable degree of **pelvic tilt**, whereby the seat bones urge the horse more forward.
4) **Bracing** the back *temporarily*, during the execution of any rebalancing half-halts, as needed.

With this attitude the seat is held more emphatically into the front of the saddle, and the weight influence comes more from the back of the seat bones. The optimum driving influence comes from the combined use of the seat in conjunction with a concurrent and equal amount of 'forward-drawing' pressure from the front line. *The more the seat bones lead, the more the front line (solar plexus/navel) must lead.*

024 Points of Non-driving Attitude of the Seat

1) Upper body leaning forward, and/or
2) completely soft, relaxed lower back, and/or

3) lower back deliberately hollowed.
4) The forward seat (two–point, jumping posture); the rider's seat is taken completely out of the saddle.

With this attitude the seat is made lighter; the rider's centre of balance falls more towards the front of the seat bones and the crotch.

025 Incorrect Attitudes of the Seat and Position

— Head nodding; looking down; nape of neck hollowed, chin sticking out.
— Shoulders rounded, heaving.
— Back hunched; collapsed upper body, caved–in front line, pulled–back stomach.[20]
— Upper body leaning forward or backward.
— Much pelvic movement; loose, 'doughy' seat, stomach flopping.
— Unquiet knees, opened away from saddle; loose, rolling thighs.
— Sitting mainly on the thighs, or seat muscles.
— Sitting more on only one seat bone.
— Sitting in the back of the saddle, being pushed along by the cantle.
— Exaggerated tapping with lower legs; heels drawn up.
— Any rigidity, stiffness, or tensions. These result in the seat bouncing in the saddle, and unquiet hands that flap up and down.
— Any visible pushing, pumping, shoving, wiping motions of the seat on the saddle.
— Any obvious use of physical power to move the horse.

[20] Instead of the desired capital 'D', the rider produces *the cursed capital 'C'*!

026 Timing of the Driving Aid from the Legs[21]

The best moments at which to ask the horse for an increase of activity are just before the hind leg is about to come off the ground, which is the moment of thrusting-off, and during the first moments when it is in the air. It cannot react as readily or effectively to driving aids during the *early* weight-bearing phase of the stride.

At the walk: Both the rider's legs actively animate the corresponding hind leg of the horse. It is an alternating left-right leg aid.[22] As we feel the horse's rib-cage filling (gently bumping) alternately against our calves, that is the right time for the aid.

At the trot and canter: The rider's inside leg gives the aid actively; the outside leg gives the same pressure but remains passive. *The importance of this equal but passive driving with the outside leg cannot be over-emphasized, though it is commonly neglected.* In exceptional cases, when a strong driving aid is needed, both legs may drive actively as a temporary corrective measure. At the trot, as at the walk, the aid is given when we feel the horse's rib-cage bulge or bump against our leg. At the canter, the driving aid should be given as the horse's neck rises up towards the rider.

027 Important Factors in Activating the Horse

In the ability to activate lies one of the most important fundamental requirements of the riding task. Only when we can:

---

[21] Always remember to consider the appropriate driving attitude from the seat/position while actively driving (tuning) the horse with the legs. Furthermore, the allowing attitude of the hands is essential so as to avoid contradictory influences during driving.

[22] Only use this active aiding when necessary, not just for good measure, or the horse will be readily dulled.

(a) *initiate* the true forward urge;
(b) *allow* it to occur with an appropriate giving hand attitude;
(c) *go with* the horse's movements with a harmonious seat and
    position, will we actually control the horse correctly.

When the horse goes truly forward, a multitude of evasions and problems are automatically eradicated. Though it is true that tensions and resistance can be 'driven out the front', this has nothing to do with ruthlessly chasing the horse forward, helter-skelter, without regard for rhythm, balance or suppleness. The following points give guidance:

— Avoid driving the horse more than it can accept, or tensions and loss of balance will result.

— As is commonly known, true work does not begin until the horse becomes relaxed to the extent that it *needs* to be driven, and *allows* itself to be driven. We must not mistake nervous or excited energy for true forward impulse. The horse must first be mentally at ease (accepting the rider) and physically relaxed (manifested in a good, relaxed, deep rhythm) before it is useful to ask for more animated stepping from behind.

— If we force the horse forward despite its hard, hollow back, we will only cause the horse to resist more and find evasions in crookedness, rushing, or constrained forward motions ('sucking back').

— The activating aids should not degenerate into a physical moving of the horse. It should be an effortless task to send the horse on, once it is put correctly on the aids. The rider should have the clear mental intention whilst activating of first, balancing the horse (think of filling a beach ball under the saddle), and second, flowing forward (think of attaining a longer stride and/or a rounder motion while remaining in the same rhythm, using the half-halt principle, see 060).

Note: See sections 068, 069, 070 for detailed indications of the horse's acceptance or rejection of the aids.

028 Tuning the Horse to Aids from the Seat and Legs

1) The correct aid from the seat/position and legs has been given ... the horse responds sluggishly.
2) *Instantly* increase the intensity of the *active*, pulsing leg aid (well based in good seat/front line attitudes), and *simultaneously* reinforce the aid with the use of stick or spur(s),[23] sufficiently that an adequate response is achieved.[24] *Do not use the stick or spurs without simultaneously engaging the natural leg aid.*
3) The moment the horse responds, neutralize the leg, and praise it with voice or a pat on the neck.
4) The next time, renew the aid with the seat and legs alone, giving the horse a chance to show its willingness.
5) This sequence is to be repeated until the horse responds willingly, without the need for back-up from the artificial aids.

Ideally, the stick should be used for supporting the driving aids, and the spurs for reinforcing the sideways-yielding and/or bending aids. Their use is dependent on each horse's individual reactions, however, and could be interchanged under certain circumstance.

Furthermore, it is essential to realize that the leg/stick are the only means by which the rider can tune the horse to the more subtle influences from the seat/position, which should ultimately be the major communicator of all the rider's intentions to the horse.

029 How to Hold and Use the Stick

— The stick is held diagonally through the hand.

---

[23] This 'tuning' must **not** become a form of punishment, nor have an attitude of 'judgement' towards the horse, but must rather be done with a kind, neutral heart, as a corrective reminder, and as a form of greater encouragement.

[24] This concept should not be used when a horse is shying. This only pertains to horses which are calm but not responding well to the aids. For more details on how to handle shying see 072.

— Do not brace the thumb against the stick: this makes for a less sensitive hand. Only the reins should be held between the thumb and the index finger, not the stick.

— The stick should be used in such a manner that we in no way disturb the horse's mouth.

— We must learn to use the stick as though it were a living extension of our hand and fingers, making a habit of feeling the horse's side through the stick before we use it. It is also useful to know how to rub the stick back and forth along the horse's side, to desensitize horses which are over-sensitive to the stick. While doing this we should apply some pressure on the stick, causing its shaft to be flexed a little, to avoid accidentally tickling the horse. If the horse does become startled, it is crucial that we do not react to this in any way, and that we nonchalantly and elastically keep the stick rubbing back and forth. While desensitizing the horse to the stick, we can use to good effect all of the attitudes relevant to shying (see 072).

— Introduce the stick on the horse's side before using it. To surprise the horse with it by using it 'out of the blue' only causes tensions, nervousness, and distrust, and an incorrect forwardness based on fear instead of understanding. We must always *earn and maintain* the horse's trust in all the aids and implements we use.

— Use the stick with little 'taps',[25] not with 'whippy', or 'stinging' flicks. (These only cause annoyance, mental resistance and tension in the horse.)

— The stick needs to be used with great eloquence, to help encourage the horse, and not as a stupid, blunt instrument.[26]

— Horses look straight through pretence – we must not *threaten* to use the stick. Either use it (frankly *but judiciously*) or don't use it.

---

[25] If necessary TAP LOUDER, but don't sting the horse.
[26] Only *extremely* rarely as a punishment. See 004: 22 and 073.

030 Quality of the Rein Contact

(a) Soft and light.
(b) Elastic at all times.
(c) Even though the contact may need to become heavier for brief moments, when passively offering the horse resistance (the *sustaining* hand), it should not become hard.

The rein aids must be transmitted through an *even, continuous, elastic, living* contact, not from a slack, flapping 'washing line'.

The softness, elasticity and sensitivity of the living contact originate from a balanced seat and an entirely independent upper body, and are transmitted through supple, relaxed shoulders, elbows and wrists to the friendly hands; such as a pleasant handshake between people. The limp, opened little hand that holds the reins towards the fingertips is to be avoided (it is a false notion of softness and, furthermore, leads to continuous slipping of the reins). We should think of the reins as starting at the elbows. The elbow is the conversion point of the energy, and transfers the energy that the horse puts into the reins directly through the rider's spine and to the horse's back once more via the seat bones. This effect can only be properly achieved with correct attitudes of the seat and upper body. The main points bear repeating here, since they are indispensable elements to achieving a *living*, elastic contact: (a) long front line; (b) shoulders back and down; (c) bent, pointy, heavy elbow; (d) ride hips (and horse) through elbows (see 009).

Note: Just as the correct seat is made up 'half-and-half' by the horse and rider,[27] so too is the contact. Even when the horse is not yet going correctly, *we must make sure that our 50 per cent of the contact is correctly established.* Any contact, and any rein aids, must be based on the horse's acceptance of the driving aids. Then, through working the horse appropriately by encouraging it to reach *evenly* into both reins in response to those forward driving aids, we assist

[27] See 007.

it to fulfil its 50 per cent. Only then is the contact 'completed' and real. (See 'completion of the circuit', 041).

031 Quality, Quantity and Intonation of the Aids

Anyone can sit on a horse … pull on the reins … squeeze with the legs … or hit the horse with the whip. This, in itself, obviously doesn't make one a good or effective rider.

The main task in all the years of learning how to administer correct aids is encompassed in the discovering of *how much*. Not only must we dispense, like a pharmacist, exactly the right 'medication', in just the right amount, at just the right time, to the right patient, but the quality and texture of each aid also plays a decisive role.

Horses have an uncanny talent for perceiving the most subtle nuances, even those that are subconsciously transmitted by the rider. Therefore, if we learn to channel these mental intentions deliberately, it facilitates a completely new horizon of highly refined communication with the creature.

In the telling of jokes lies an example of the intonation which can colour the aids. The words alone, however clever they might be, play only a relatively small part in the presentation of wit. When the feeling for suitable expression, gesture and timing is lacking, the joke falls flat. Similarly with the giving of aids, one can either fail or succeed, depending frequently only on this talent for appropriate timing and inflection; this embodies the full spectrum of equestrian tact and feeling.

032 Sequence of Changing Position and Aids when Changing the Bend

Though the position is a rapid sequence, one should follow this order.

1) CHANGE THE SEAT: The new inside seat bone must have a

greater forward emphasis, and with a little more weight in it.[28] This extra weight must also flow down through a more deeply emphasized inside knee and stirrup iron, and with the energy pattern flowing down through the heel to the ground.

2) CHANGE THE DRIVING LEG: The horse must be bent around the rider's *new* inside leg which should act like a *passive* post. It takes on this role as 'post' for the *new* bend *before* the bend can be changed, and is a preparation for that event. It also gives the active driving aid. As the legs are changed, slide them along the horse's sides; do not take them off while repositioning them. Always make a clear distinction when changing the leg positions: the inside leg at the normal position near the girth, and the outside leg held back (approximately a hand's breath), passively supporting the quarters from swinging out.

3) CHANGE THE BENDING REIN AIDS: These will only be obeyed when balance and forwardness have been maintained, and the seat and leg aids have been correct. The bending rein aids should always be given in an elastic, asking manner.

— **Helpful hint:** while taking care to maintain the balance and an even rhythm, think of the *new* inside leg, and the *new* outside rein *before* and during all changes of rein (or the bend).

033 Essential Points for Correct Bending

— Implement all bending influences with a predominating forward intention. Drive the horse into the new direction. Always strive to keep the gaits pure, correct, and fluid.
— Keep the horse *tracking* straight (single track work 035: 3).
— Increase the weight on the inside seat bone, and down through the knee, as you turn the upper body[29] and direct its energy through the new inside window (009; 'three windows' concept).

---

[28] This should **not** be achieved by taking weight off the outside seat bone; nor should the outside seat bone be allowed to drift backward.
[29] We need to take care, however, not to lean, collapse, or warp the body in any way.

— Adjust the seat and legs: inside leg at the girth; outside leg a hand's breadth further back (032).
— Elastically ask the horse to *look* in with the inside rein; flexing it behind the jaw/ear.
— Do not overbend the horse's neck – that is, beyond seeing only a *glimpse* of the inside eye and nostril rim – especially not at its base.
— Play out the outside rein *slightly* without losing the contact or letting the horse escape out of the outside shoulder. This is a 'feeling' rather than an overt act.
— *New inside leg, and new outside rein are the main players on the scene to achieve the bend in the horse's body.*
— The maintenance of a continuous, *elastic*, 'counterbalancing interaction' between the inside and outside rein is essential. Real bending comes from the ability to 'feel' the horse into it with the full orchestra of the aids.
— Maintain the horse's balance (even rhythm and correct tempo), preventing the horse from rushing away from the bending influence (half-halt if necessary).

Be sure that the poll remains the highest point, and that the horse's ears remain on the same level during bending. It is a common error for the nose to tip inward and the horse's outside ear to drop down because of an incorrect, dominant inside rein, combined with a lack of forward energy from the inside leg (see 038: e).

If a horse shows resistance to bending, it is entirely unhelpful for the rider to try to force the bend with strong active, backward aids on the inside rein (though it may be mighty tempting to do so!). It is important to realize that horses are very rarely stubborn. Usually the causes for difficult bending lie elsewhere. Here are some of the most common causes:

– the horse it is not balanced
– it is not using both hind legs evenly, and therefore isn't reaching into both reins evenly
– it is mentally upset.

The solution lies in understanding that the resistant side is not actually the difficult side at all. The problem can be solved by encouraging the horse to stretch (reach) better for the rein on the *lighter* side. It will be found that once the horse is reaching for that lighter rein better ('filling' it), it will, apparently miraculously, bend without problem towards the stiff or resistant side. *In other words, we must help the horse to stretch into both reins evenly* through the appropriate use of the driving aids (see 045).

— When the horse does yield to the bend, the rider too must instantly equalize the pressure of both reins, becoming totally neutral in that bent state, and must refresh the horse's forwardness with the driving aids while giving with the hands.

— Only if the horse should voluntarily try to straighten, against the rider's wishes, or if the rider expressly wants to alter the bend, should any further bending aids be given.[30]

— Besides bending the horse through its body, most of the bend in the neck should take place towards its top end (behind the ears/jaw especially) and not at its base by the shoulders. The withers and shoulders must be well 'framed' between the reins, so that the horse's energy always arrives at the bridle, and doesn't leak out through the outside shoulder, nor cut in at the inside shoulder.

— After bending has take place the horse must be reaching softly, elastically and *evenly into **both** reins!* If the horse is 'empty' on the inside rein, only a 'false' bend will have been achieved.[31]

— We know that our inside leg is to be a *passive* post during bending. However, there are circumstances in which we may need to use it *momentarily* actively: (a) when the horse stiffens against the leg during bending attempts, (b) when

---

[30] To be strictly avoided is the constant fiddling with the inside rein. It only dulls the horse, and does not produce a correct bending attitude through the horse. It ends up with a cramping, shortening, of the inside of the horse, instead of a fluid, even reaching while bending.

[31] Unless the horse reaches constantly for the inside rein it is not correctly 'on the aids'.

the horse wants to cut in instead of bend. In both cases, all the active leg needs to achieve is to indicate to the horse to respect the leg's passive presence, and not stiffen or cut in against it.

— 'Bending' and 'guiding' are, unequivocally, to be seen as mutually exclusive concepts. When bending we must not change the school figure we are on. When guiding (steering) we must not change the bend.

— The two circumstances under which we should strictly *not* change the bend are: (a) while guiding, and (b) while half-halting.

— The only conditions under which we *may* change the bend are (a) when *deliberately* bending (or changing the bend), and (b) when *deliberately* straightening the horse. (Though this pertains to the bend in the whole horse, it is especially crucial with respect to the neck.)

Ideally, through suitable training, all bending should be attained through a subtle, and wholly passive, creamy and smooth, 'lateral forming in forwardness' of the horse from seat/leg and position attitudes. Further-more, at the risk of stating the obvious, it is imperative to stress that the horse must actually *soften* to the bending aids, forming a *living* bend (a common problem being that the horse may well be bent but that it has not yielded willingly, in which case it will merely have formed a dead, concrete arc.)

034 How Does the Disease 'Inside-Rein-itis' Manifest Itself?

Through the incorrect, direct use of the inside rein the rider attempts to:

— Pull the horse onto circles with it.
— Pull the horse through corners with it.
— 'Steer' with it.
— Pull the horse into shoulder-in with it.

— Do turns on the haunches with it.
— Make the horse leg-yield or do turns on the forehand with it.
— Generally keep the horse from cutting-in by pressing the inside rein against the neck (instead of using the inside leg).

Avoid, like death itself, any of the above misuses of the inside rein! The rider must learn to guide (or 'steer') the horse mainly with the seat and legs (driving the horse in the required direction), and with the outside rein.[32] In the above-mentioned circumstances, the reins should play largely only a *framing* role.

What may the inside rein do?

— The inside rein may be used to **bend** the horse; that is, *flex* it at the tip of the 'fishing rod', not at its base (it should *not* be used to **turn**, or 'steer' the horse).
— It may be used to 'lead' the horse inward by opening the inside hand away from the neck, while the outside rein *gently* yet clearly keeps the neck 'stable', that is, from overbending. This method is used especially with young horses which haven't yet learned how to reach into both reins evenly, and don't yet understand the guiding function of the outside rein.

Turning the horse becomes easy and automatic once we have learned how to balance the horse, and form it laterally by bending the channel made up of our legs and reins. *When the horse is balanced*, then all we need to do is to send the horse forward through that bent channel. If the horse steers like a pig, it isn't going forward, nor is it balanced. (See 038, framing the horse.)

Reflections III

— Expect, and get, responses from every aid, every time.
— Only a truly supple, relaxed, balanced horse can correctly obey a rein aid.

---

[32] Even weight in both reins anyway!

— Our reactions must be lightening-quick, but our attitude towards the horse should be as though we had all the time in the world. It is a calmness that seems at odds with the speed of reaction.

— We achieve best results when we ourselves are reasonably prepared, mentally and physically, before asking the horse for anything.

— It must be our chief aim to cause the horse to respond to ever-lighter aids.

— It is a serious fault to ride the horse with the whip or spurs only, without first having given the aid honestly with the seat/position and legs.

— It is unproductive to ambush or surprise the horse with any aid.

— The seat bone, leg, and rein of the rider on one side, react directly with the corresponding hind leg of the horse.

— The energy which is generated by the leg in pounds … should be received by the hand in ounces.[33]

— No aids will more adversely affect the horse than harsh, unfeeling rein aids.

— Only once the rider becomes quiet will the horse be able to hear the whispers of the finer aids.

— The hands must give the hind legs space to step; they should have a giving attitude towards the horse's mouth. This does not necessarily mean always to give the reins away *measurably*; it can also be just an *attitude* of yielding or allowing.

— Having a clear mental intention while giving any aid helps us avoid turning our riding into a strictly physical task.

— The most misused aid is the inside rein. The most neglected aid is the outside leg.

— 'Sawing' with the hands is equestrian cancer.

---

[33] Egon von Neindorff.

Barty. 'Forward and down' at the working trot.

CHAPTER IV

Working the Horse

Concepts

— Measure of good riding? ... quietness, harmony – elegance.
— We mustn't do things *to* the horse, but rather together, *with* it.
— Give the horse time to accept our presence before making requests.
— Through balanced forwardness the 'river-banks' become watertight.
— No credit ... first put energy in the 'piggy bank' ... then spend.
— Horse two-thirds in front of us, one third behind.[1]
— Foundation ... always keep the horse reaching for the bridle.

Guidelines

— Serenity
— Feeling
— Participation
— Harmony

---

[1] Like the bow wave of a boat.

035 Principles of Riding

1) CALM: —   Calm is the first principle, because without it a horse is in no state to listen to the rider: it is not approachable.

           —   The horse is calm when it is mentally at ease, in an unagitated, cooperative state of mind, whereby it allows its energies to be usefully directed by the rider. It does not mean that the horse is a dullard.

           —   The horse is not calm when:

             (a) Adversely affected by outside stimuli; this includes the rider.

             (b) 'High' from being in the stable for an extended period; overfeeding of grain combined with insufficient work ('stable-mental').

             (c) When it has a nervous temperament.

2) FORWARD: —   When forwardness is present, the horse uses *more* energy than it needs to get from 'A' to 'B', and through the rider's influences this excess energy is converted into supple, balanced gaits, which show an active, correct, and even rhythm. It is an energetic, unconstrained, fluid motion, neither rushing nor lazy. It is the basis on which all honest work is built.

           —   Rushing means that the horse is going in too fast a rhythm; 'chasing', unbalanced, on the forehand; or the horse is running on tension or fear.

           —   Lazy means, the horse may well be in the correct rhythm but isn't active from behind; a dull, expressionless, unbalanced motion.

3) STRAIGHT: —   Straight work is referred to as work on a *single track*.

                           — A horse is *technically* straight when its hind feet travel *within* the same path as its front feet.

                           — Within the above requirement, the horse's spine and neck must also be bent exactly on the form of the line or figure being ridden. (Counter-bend and two-track exercises excepted.)

                           — True *dynamic* straightness further requires that the horse is correctly 'on the aids': that through suppleness and activity the horse accepts (reaches for) both sides of the bit equally – a genuine state of self-carriage; a dynamic balance in which both the lateral and longitudinal pairs of legs are equally loaded throughout all exercises, both in single- and two-track work.

Note: The volte is the smallest curved line (6m) on which the horse is able to form its body. If the rider wishes to make smaller turns, then correct two-track work must be used, culminating in turns on the haunches.

036 Six Major Guidelines for Correct Riding and Training

— Rhythm
— Relaxation[2]
— Contact
— Straightness
— Impulsion
— Collection

[2] Suppleness. In German, *Losgelassenheit* … a state of having 'let go'; easy, swinging, flowing, fluid.

It must be noted that these are individual, successive stages of riding or training. One must achieve each single requirement before the next step can be attained. There must be an even, correct rhythm before suppleness will be reached; only a supple horse will manifest a correct contact, which the horse searches for and takes up; after which straightening can easily be attained; only then can the rider ask for more impulsion, which, after the appropriate amount of physical conditioning, can be furthered to a true collection. It is interesting to note, however, that the first four of these points frequently appear nearly all at once; they are very closely inter-related.

037 Fundamental Aims in Training the Horse

— Initial handling and longeing sessions to acquaint the youngster with the bridle, saddle, and tack; these are the first simple obedience lessons.[3]
— The horse gradually becomes accustomed to the carrying and balancing of the rider's weight on a supple, elastic back.
— The horse is encouraged to cooperate with the rider's wishes – willing responsiveness, accuracy in performance of school figures and execution of exercises. If the horse is not over-faced, obedience poses few problems, and only minimal time needs to be spent exclusively on it. Every aid could be seen as a small obedience or 'tuning' lesson.[4]
— Gymnastic training; the building of muscle, tendons, heart and lungs for strength and endurance, and the full development of the balance, ambidexterity and athletic qualities of the horse under saddle. The greatest skill,

---

[3] Though it seems simple to us, for the horse this is a momentous experience to allow its freedom of choice, and its natural energies, to become structured and controlled for the first time, so it is essential that we don't take the horse's compliance for granted: encourage and praise it.

[4] Obedience as such is not the most important issue, however, and care must be taken because it can all too easily degenerate into a 'soulless submission'. We need to *help* the horse to 'understand' what we want, and thereby access its generosity and willing cooperation.

experience, and time in training are spent on this work. Yet, such technical gymnastics can only bring good quality results when the rider's heart/mentality/philosophical outlook is sound.[5]

— Gradually and systematically, as the horse becomes able to cope with the work, the more advanced exercises are introduced without causing either physical or psychological damage.

When the horse is carefully steeped in a consistent routine, handled with firm kindness and respect, it becomes mentally mature and mellowed … a willing and generous worker, strong in self-confidence, and trusting in our human leadership.

038 Framing the Horse

— In order to gain precise control the rider must *frame* the horse.

— To frame means to *contain and align* the horse within the clear perimeter of the rider's natural tools: the seat,[6] legs, and hands (reins). (See 020).

— The rider's legs (containing the horse's shoulders, body and quarters) and reins (containing the horse's head, neck and shoulders[7]) must form a channel, like two river-banks, through which the horse is allowed to flow forward. The left seat bone, rein and leg contain the left side, the right seat bone, rein and leg contain the right side. *Only forwardness, converted into balance under the seat, can make the river-banks truly water (energy) proof.*

---

[5] It is possible to 'technicalize' one's way all the way up to Grand Prix, without an ounce of sense (read 'heart') for the horse. One ends up with hair-trigger responsiveness and accuracy, but the horse's eagerness, its 'horseness' has departed, and we end with a soulless automaton, which responds either out of 'hammered-in' habit, or out of fear. We need to ask ourselves the serious question: 'Is that truly the noble, dignified form of horsemanship to which we aspire?'

[6] Though the legs and reins are the main 'framing' agents, without the seat bones being steadily and evenly on the saddle correct framing is greatly compromised.

[7] Take note that the horse's shoulders are an area where the 'containing duties' overlap; partially contained by the legs, and partially *though mainly* contained by the reins. Independent balance of the horse is the best 'containing agent' of all.

— Both seat bones, both legs and both reins must have a continuous contact with the horse.

If the contact of any one of these is lacking, then the horse is no longer framed, giving it a hole through which its energy can escape. Crookedness may result, and also poor control over the rhythm, activity, alignment and balance. It is particularly essential that both reins stabilize the base of the neck onto the withers and shoulders, quietly and passively preventing any lateral snakiness of the neck at this location.

Even if the rider has a contact with both seat bones, reins and legs, there are more subtle ways in which the animal is not framed. These are some of the common difficulties:

(a) Opening or crossing the jaw. (Can be prevented by appropriate adjustment of the noseband [not too tight!! – the horse must still be able to chew comfortably]; and riding with a light hand while sending the horse forward.)

(b) Drawing–up or sticking-out of the tongue. (The result of riding with hard, dominating, active or dead hands. Forced riding.)

(c) The base of the horse's neck is bent, laterally, more than the curve of the line being ridden. This prevails when we have not bent the horse evenly throughout its body. The neck is overbent, being broken sideways just ahead of the withers. The horse's energy escapes us by falling out through the outside shoulder, or running-out. (Can be prevented, first, by straightening the horse's neck, and by improving the balance of the horse by realigning its outside shoulder with the croup once again.) We need to be aware of the function of the outside rein and leg as a *passive* containing/straightening wall. If the horse does not respect that wall,[8] it needs to be rebalanced in forwardness.

(d) The horse's neck is broken or kinked at the third vertebra behind the poll. This is a very serious fault, since the horse has effectively come behind the bit. The neck and spinal column are no longer a continuous unit and thus the forehand and

---

[8] Just using a loud, active outside leg to overcome this is usually not productive.

hindquarters are not united. The basic requirement for putting the horse correctly 'on the aids' no longer exists, and the location of the horse's head is not relevant to its way of going. This is usually a result of forced riding; the horse's head has been pulled down without regard for its natural balance. (Can be corrected by bold forward riding [maintain the rhythm, balance], and the forward and downward exercise, see 045.)

(e) The horse tipping its head sideways, warping its neck. The ears are no longer on the same level (see photograph on p108). Can be a result of forced riding; a lack of forward urge; unequal pressure in the reins; the horse is bottled–up, tense. (Besides riding the horse more energetically forward, this can be corrected by driving more with the leg on the 'empty' side, while *thinking* of [that is *passively* sustaining] the rein on the resistant side. To effect the correction, it is best to have little or no bend in the neck until the horse is reaching evenly into the reins once again.)

039 Framing Function of the Seat

By sitting down correctly the rider is able to hold the horse between the seat bones, and in front of the seat and leg. This directly influences the presence of the hindquarters underneath the seat, and prevents the horse from going in a broken–apart manner. 'He who has control of the hind foot of the horse, controls the whole horse.'[9] (See 008, 021.)

040 Criteria for the Correct Head Position of the Horse

1) Poll the highest skeletal point of the whole horse.
2) Nose slightly ahead of, or on the vertical line.[10]
3) Ears on the same level.

[9] Egon von Neindorff.
[10] NEVER behind the vertical, period!

041 Completion of the Circuit

The circuit can only be complete if both horse and rider are entirely void of tensions and resistance. Furthermore, correctness of the rider's seat and position are essential to successful completion of the circuit (see 009). Only through suppleness can the horse's energy flow unimpeded through its whole body, whereby the hindquarters can react correctly to the driving aids and begin to carry more weight (044). This entails the correct use of the horse's 'muscle ring' (that is, the back, stomach, and neck muscles are harmoniously in play), and the extensors and flexors working in an unforced, balanced way.

The rider, being the motivator of the action, causes the horse to step actively through its back. The impulse travels through the horse's spine, neck, poll and jaw to the bit, then through the reins into the rider's hands, elbows, shoulders and down the rider's spine, which then reacts directly, via the seat bones, on the horse's back once more. This completion of the circuit (when the energy generated through the rider's seat and leg influences arrives back in the hands via the supple, forward-going, *reaching* horse: 'leg in hand') is the basis for all correct work.

042 'On the Aids' Versus 'Collection'

The term 'collection' is quite often mistakenly interchanged with 'on the aids'. Though the horse does indeed 'gather itself up' under the rider when it is put 'on the aids', there is an important difference between these two concepts. Here is a brief description.

To put a horse 'on the aids' means bringing it into a balanced, carrying, accepting state. *As a consequence* the horse yields at the poll, chews on the bit, and finds the correct head position. It is a 'cat-poised-to-pounce-on-a-mouse' state of willing readiness under the rider, and is the foundation for all correct work. A horse which is 'on the aids' is thereby prepared to do anything (depending, of course, on its individual level of training) which would include the extremes of the spectrum, both extension *and* collection of the three gaits.

Collection itself, however, is a state attained only after many years of patient, systematic, gymnastic work, which is made evident in a shorter, higher, rounder, *more active* stride. It is to be attained solely through a greater balancing of the horse on the hindquarters, *based on forward impulse* – and not merely by shortening up the horse from the front. The horse's motion must remain forward, fluid, and energetic, and must always continue to show the correct sequence of footfall in all gaits (053, 055, 056). The hallmark of true collection is a *clear lowering of the croup*, brought about by the deeply bent, engaged haunches that carry more weight. This deep bending gives good collected work (despite its increased vigour) the distinction of uncanny quietness – a soft, elastic power – made possible through the flexing of the three major joints; hip, stifle, and hock. This also gives the horse a true 'uphill' quality in its way of going – two-thirds of the horse in front of the rider, one third behind. Fortunately, this cannot be falsified and it requires willing participation and contribution from the horse. The use of 'quick-fix' methods to achieve unmerited collection is probably one of the most common causes of resistances, disharmony, and lameness in the horse.

043 What Does 'On The Aids' Mean?

As mentioned earlier, 'on the aids' is a state of poised readiness in the horse. The horse which is being ridden on a loose rein is like a bow which has not yet been strung: one cannot quickly or effectively shoot arrows with it. When the horse is put 'on the aids', it becomes balanced and its body becomes like a compressed spring – the strung bow. The compression occurs when the horse obeys the activating aids and commences to step impulsively through its back, and consequently begins to stretch its whole body for the bit. As it finds resistance at the bit (because the rider *momentarily* and passively 'sustains' the pressure the horse puts in the reins – generated by the driving aids), the horse's neck rises up off the withers, and the forward energy is converted into a balanced, 'carrying' energy under the saddle. This conversion can occur only if the horse yields willingly at the poll (this should in no way be forced). From this series of events the hindquarters become more loaded, and the centre of balance moves back, beneath the rider's seat. Subsequently the horse also finds a suitable, natural head position that is in harmony with its way of going. When this state can be maintained in all three gaits and through all simple school figures and transitions, then the horse can be considered to be well 'on the aids'.

It is particularly through the unification of the horse's and rider's centres of balance, the result of a correct 'putting on the aids', that the horse becomes liberated, and this enables it to respond easily and instantly to the rider's wishes. Only once this coinciding of centres of balance materializes, do the weight aids find their true impact.

When the young horse is put on the aids, the neck rises very gently up off the withers, and the nose is still well in front of the vertical. With more advanced horses, which have gained in physical fitness, and have improved in their balance, suppleness and activity, the neck rises more markedly up from the withers, and the nose comes closer to the vertical. *The correct head position (040) is a symptom, which has value only when it is the **end result** of the horse balancing itself by stepping actively through its back.*

The head and neck position of the horse could be seen as a barometer, indicating the state of the horse's way of going. So long as the rider works in accordance with correct, natural principles, this barometer is an accurate guide. If, however, incorrect methods are used (placing the head and neck artificially), the barometer shows a false reading: it indicates that the weather is 85°F and sunny when, in actual fact, it might be 40° below zero with a blizzard going on – clearly a fool's paradise!

044 How is the Horse Put 'On The Aids?

The following description is based on the premise that we are dealing with a reasonably well-trained horse, at a basic level.

This being the fundamental state from which all work commences, it is essential that the rider learns to put the horse 'on the aids' efficiently. In order to do so, the rider needs to have the horse nicely 'tuned' to (responsive to):

– the forward driving aids;
– the bending aids;[11]
– the sideways-yielding aids from the legs.

As a result of willing responsiveness to these three categories of aids, the horse will consequently begin to accept the rein influences. Remember, the reins play largely a *passive, receiving* role. It is also important to note that the correct lateral bend (flexion), and the longitudinal yielding (the horse's giving in its back/neck/poll) occur wholly in conjunction with one another. Neither is complete without the other, and the successful completion of both is reliant on the liberating effect of the horse's balance under the saddle. Independent balance is the most important product of putting the horse 'on the aids'. To achieve this the driving and receiving influences must be in a state of continuous, harmonious interaction.

— The horse can be put on the aids at the walk (young horses excepted, see 053), by riding accurate 10m circles or voltes,[12] and curved lines with fairly frequent changes of rein (see 066).
— We must properly 'frame' the horse within the perimeter of our aids (see 037).
— We must offer the horse an even, elastic contact.
— It is essential to maintain an absolutely even, correct rhythm, so that the energy we generate can be converted into carrying instead of rushing; the half-halt plays an important role (060). Use a *filtering* hand, not a blocking one.
— While putting the horse 'on the aids', the rider must, to the necessary extent, tactfully excite impulsive forward stepping from the hindquarters, animating the horse to reach into both reins. (This active driving is immediately lessened [or stopped] once the horse comes on the aids and has found its balance – self-carriage.)

[11] Do not bend the horse beyond the point where you can see a glimpse of the inside eye and nostril rim.
[12] The accurate size and location of the school figure are crucial to success.

Only through tactfulness and sensitivity can a favourable response be expected from the horse. In the appropriate ratio and relationship between the activating aids from the seat and legs, and the suitable receiving, filtering, sustaining (or timely yielding) attitudes of the hands, lies the key to influencing the increased loading of the hindquarters, and therefore the balance of the horse. This balanced state must be born out of the forward impulse of the gaits; referred to as **relative erection** of the head and neck. It can only be correctly achieved and maintained through the predominant (*this does not mean continuous!*) use of the driving aids.

If the horse's head position has been achieved artificially through the direct use of an active, backward-working, predominant hand, referred to as **active erection** of the head and neck, the resulting exterior appearance of the horse will have no correlation to either the impulsion, balance, or willing compliance of the horse. (The German riding master, Julius Walzer, was known to have said, 'With the unknowledgeable rider the art starts at the horse's neck, and it also desists there!').[13]

045 Forward and Down

The forward and down exercise epitomizes one of the most important fundamentals of riding: that *in response to the forward driving aids* (see 027), the horse learns to stretch its whole spine forward in order to reach for and find the bit correctly. In conjunction with this, it is an excellent way of assisting the rider to raise and fill the horse's back and neck, which should bow upward elastically both behind and in front of the withers. The basic principle on which the exercise operates is a vital element in putting the horse correctly 'on the aids'. It underscores the importance of the horse's independent balance – that it carries itself without seeking an artificial support from the reins. Furthermore, through the exercise the rider gains the necessary

---

[13] *Meister der Reitkunst*, Waldemar Seunig, Erich Hoffmann Verlag 1960.

understanding of how to lengthen or shorten the horse's frame, either in conjunction with, or independent of, extension or collection of the gaits.

The forward and down exercise is not necessarily used only as a transitional stage in the training of young horses. One should be able to demonstrate 'forward and down' with any horse, at any stage of training. It will always remain for the rider tangible proof that the horse has been worked correctly, from back to front, and that its back muscles are elastically in play, originating from lively impulsive hindquarters.

There are three main foundation stones on which the exercise is built:

1) Even rhythm, and the resulting balance, relaxation, and freedom from constraint (see 036, logical sequence of training), so that the horse is in an accepting, 'driveable' state (027).
2) The first stage of bending: that, in answer to the driving aids, the horse stretches the *outside* of its body when the outside rein is yielded forward, while the inside rein sustains passively, *waiting* for the horse to soften to the bend.[14] Once the horse has given to the bend, the rider must then make the 'giving' *attitude* in both reins absolutely even, while encouraging the horse to reach evenly into them with the driving aids.[15]
3) Accurate riding of school figures (type, size, and location) is essential to success.

Initially, the young horse should be allowed and encouraged to stretch 'forward and down' at any time it wishes. Once it begins to

[14] This would be considered a very rudimentary form of bending, called 'passive bending'. While giving on the outside rein, care must be taken not to lose the horse's balance, nor its straightness (alignment), by letting its energy spill out at the outside shoulder. If the horse should cut out at the shoulder, judicious half-halts on the outside rein, in conjunction with suitable driving from the inside leg, are essential to regaining both the horse's alignment and its independent balance. If the half-halts have succeeded, the horse will want to go directly towards where its nose is pointing (instead of running out) when *both* reins are given *evenly* forward towards the horse's mouth while driving.

[15] Unless the horse is reaching into BOTH reins, it is not truly *alive* 'on the aids'. It should neither lean on, nor evade stretching for, *either* rein.

Barty. 'Forward and down' at the working canter left.

get the idea, however, it should only be allowed down at the rider's request.[16] As the rider gradually begins to yield forward with the reins (straight towards the horse's mouth only; not up the mane towards the horse's ears, nor down to the rider's knees), care must be taken to keep the contact, and an even rhythm, while encouraging the horse with the driving aids to continue to stretch for the bit all the way down to the ground. *The horse's nose must remain at, or in front of, the vertical at all times.*

---

[16] With some naturally well-balanced horses, this may be within a few days; with unbalanced or spoiled horses, or those of poor conformation, it could take a month or more before the horse stretches well and confidently enough.

One can easily either (a) prevent the horse from going down, or (b) bring the horse's head back up to the correct position (with the poll as the highest point), by increasing the driving, while maintaining the rhythm (060, the half-halt principle).

For both horse and rider, the exercise is best learned at the trot (rising for young horses). Once familiarity has been gained, the forward and down exercise can be practised at the walk and canter as well. Barring extenuating circumstances, with older horses the exercise could be done with a full seat in all three gaits.

The exercise is best carried out by using large, simple school figures; those which will not interfere with the smooth continuity of the work. At first it is best to use a 20m circle, changing the rein *out* of the circle every fourth or fifth time round. If the horse is prone to rushing, put it on a smaller circle until it accepts the driving aids, indicated by the rhythm becoming more deep and steady because its back has become more relaxed. The circle should be enlarged once again when the horse becomes 'driveable'. Keep the following points in mind:

— Keep an even, correct rhythm (relaxed, calm, accepting horse).
— Carefully drive the horse into lengthening its body, and stretching its neck to the ground. *The forward urge is the main ingredient of success.*
— The horse must have yielded to the bend by stretching the outside of its body and neck. It should not be against the inside rein, nor try to straighten its neck, nor should it begin to lean in against the inside leg, when it is allowed to stretch.[17] It should also not overbend its neck to the inside, and end up falling out at the outside shoulder. It must be balanced and go independently through the channel formed by the rider's legs and reins.

---

[17] These would all be signs of lack of independent balance.

— Though the rein influences are by far secondary, we can encourage and assist the horse to find the stretching by alternately applying *subtle and passive* 'hold – soften' qualities[18] on the reins with a light, gentle hand. The contact must be even, continuous, and elastic throughout the entire exercise. The work is correct when the horse reaches evenly into both reins.

Forward and down is not meant to be an exercise that releases the horse from the rider's aids and controls, allowing it merely to dawdle along unbalanced on the forehand. Nor should it stretch either because of laxity, or because of an evasive jerking-away of the reins (barging down).

Once the rider becomes proficient at this exercise, it will be found enormously helpful to practise alternating frequently between riding 'forward and down' and putting the horse up 'on the aids'. Not only will this develop correct 'feel' in the rider, but the gaits will also blossom beautifully.

046 Equal Loading of the Horse's Legs

Besides the equal loading of front and hind legs, which balances the horse and causes it to find the correct head position in self-carriage, the legs must also be equally loaded laterally: lateral equilibrium. If the horse is properly suppled and 'on the aids', this equal lateral loading occurs automatically and naturally.

Indications of the horse *not* having the equal weight on the inside and outside legs are:

— Horse leaning more on one rein.
— Horse's body bulging against one of the rider's legs.
— Horse wanting to cut in or out.
— Horse going crooked.
— Head tipping; ears not on same level.
— Unlevel gait.

[18] This should be invisible to the observer, and certainly does not mean to fiddle actively with the bit.

The author with Auditeur, at Reitinstitut von Neindorff, 1995. Working canter left. Though quite nicely balanced, there is still a degree of unresolved tension present. Photo by E. Richter.

Reflections IV

— The finest work ensues when we act in the spirit of kindness and gracefulness towards the horse, rather than being dictatorial, mean-spirited, judgmental or retaliatory.

— Over-facing and over-exercising are common errors. When training the horse, do little and be moderate in the number of repetitions on any given day. Hurry up slowly.

— Any artificial placement of the horse's head must be strictly avoided.

— It is damaging to the horse's gaits to ride any exercise in two-track work, turns on the haunches, or any of the gait variants (that is, other than ordinary walk, trot, and canter) unless the horse is first put correctly 'on the aids'.

— It must be repeatedly impressed on each rider to instil in the horse the urge to move forward fluidly.

— Let-throughable: permeable. In German '*durchlässig*'. That state in which the horse allows the energy from the hindquarters to flow through its whole body (041). This is an integral part of true suppleness. The rider's aids are not only answered, they go *through* the whole horse.

— One will always be able to trace any riding problem to the breaking of one, or all of the cardinal rules of horsemanship: Calm, Forward, and Straight (035).

— If the horse is trained by force, force will be required to ride it.

— If the horse should become overbent (the poll low, the nose behind the vertical), the driving aids (a tap with the stick if necessary), in combination with normal half-halt attitudes, must be used to raise the head to the correct position. Do not raise the hand, nor use sharp upward jerks on the inside rein to effect this correction.

— It is essential that the moment the horse yields to the rein pressure, the rider also instantly yields and becomes lighter with the hand (017: d). The same principle applies to leg aids.

— The most difficult task the rider has to perform is to ride, purely and accurately, the three basic gaits 'on the aids'. Once this has been truly mastered, the advanced exercises are relatively easy, being a logical progression of correct basic work.

— When putting the horse 'on the aids' it is imperative to have it well on the inside leg and outside rein. This does not mean to take a heavier contact on the outside rein, nor that we should abandon the 'presence' of the other riding tools (the outside leg, inside rein).

— When in trouble: do less! Neutralize. Let the horse settle down and 'find itself'[19] before making new demands.

— We must use to our advantage an *isolation strip of time* between old, poor work and new, better work; that is, stay at the same level of simple work (a few days, or weeks, or even months) until new habits are well formed, and unwanted habits have withered away. This applies particularly to retrieving badly spoiled horses.

— Attaining obedience to seat and leg is the only genuine solution to gaining the horse's subsequent obedience and lightness to the reins.

— The faucet doesn't go down the drain with the water when we open it. So too, our hands do not necessarily have to give forward *measurably* in order to allow the horse forward. It can be just an *attitude* of giving or allowing.

— It is ever-challenging to produce a harmonious relationship between the driving and receiving aids, based on the needs of the moment.

---

[19] Become comfortable inside its own skin, and accepting of the rider's presence once more.

Atlantis. Turn on the haunches, right.

CHAPTER V

The Exercises; the Three Gaits; Two-track Work; School Figures

047 Categories of Exercises

1) **Loosening exercises: (preparatory work)**
   — walk on the loose rein
   — rising trot
   — turns on the forehand (sparingly)
   — leg-yielding (sparingly)
   — bending the horse left and right at the standstill, or while on straight lines at the walk and trot (not with young horses! – see below)
   — with some horses, an easy canter for a few minutes (light seat)
   — trot-canter-trot transitions
   — forward and down stretching (045)
   — use simple, large, open school figures; round-off the corners

2) **Suppling exercises: (actual work starts here)**
   — smaller school figures can be used: 10m circles, voltes, tighter serpentines, deeper into corners, etc.
   — frequent changes of rein
   — riding positions right and left alternately on straight lines at walk and trot
   — lengthening and shortening the stride in all three gaits

— riding transitions
— halt and rein-back
— shoulder-fore at trot and canter
— shoulder-in, and counter shoulder-in
— counter-canter

3) Collecting exercises
— shoulder-in
— travers and renvers
— turns on the haunches
— halt and rein-back
— counter-canter
— all suppling exercises can be included

4) Collected work: (The High School exercises)
— three collected gaits
— canter pirouettes
— flying changes
— piaffe and passage

5) The airs above the ground

048 Introduction: the Practical Use of Exercises

Each day the horse is worked, it should be taken systematically and progressively through the loosening, then the suppling, and finally, provided it is sufficiently advanced, the collecting exercises. It must demonstrate relaxation and willingness in each of these phases. If it does not, it should not be taken any further into more advanced or complex exercises until this basic correctness has been achieved. Furthermore, it is good practice to take the horse through a small, condensed version of its training programme to date, until those exercises are attained which are yet to be improved on, or which have yet to be introduced.

Should we find a major discrepancy between the quality of our basic schooling and our attempts at advanced work, then either the basis is as yet inadequate or incorrect, or the advanced work subscribes to false methods in an attempt to squeeze the much sought-after High School movements from an ill-prepared horse (or rider). Unless the horse can demonstrate relaxed, pleasant 'simple stuff' in each riding session, *regardless of its level of training*, it certainly will not be ready to do correct advanced work. There needs to be a smooth, predictable progression, with each advancement being well-based on solid preparatory work.

When the rider is as yet not sufficiently experienced, it is important to work with a clear, disciplined plan in mind. Though a bit of 'free' experimentation is always a healthy part of learning, too much liberty, before some sound understanding is gained, leads only to indifferent results. Only the experienced rider can afford to (seemingly) flit about without any recognizable plan, and do whatever is either necessary or possible at any given moment. This is so because such a rider has the ability to sense continued correctness of the gaits and freedom and balance in the horse, without specific reference to the apparent success or completion of any particular movement. It would be very unwise for the beginner to ride in such a manner. On the other side of the coin, even the less experienced rider should avoid working in over-set, repetitive patterns. Horses all too quickly latch on to such predictable work, and begin to anticipate and take over the leadership role.

Each riding session should be divided into suitable periods of work and rest. For unfit or young horses a rough approximation could be anywhere from five to ten minutes of work followed by five minutes of rest (walk, on the buckle), with a total riding time of about half an hour. For older and fitter horses, working periods can be expanded to fifteen or twenty minutes before resting for about five minutes, with a total riding time of about one hour.

The intermittent rest is important for the physical and mental well-being of the horse, and it also helps keep the rider's outlook fresh. With few exceptions, long, drawn-out sessions without rest tend to result in tired, inelastic muscles, and mental resistance in the horse.

It is good practice to give horses one regular day off work per week, with turnout in the paddock (more days off for young horses.[1]) Also, whenever possible, periodic hacking in the countryside is most beneficial for horse and rider.

049 Elaboration on the Loosening Exercises (047:1)

The main objective of the loosening phase is to let the horse find itself: allowing it to settle in; to become at ease with and accepting of the rider's weight on its back; and to rid its body of stiffness or discomfort from being in the stable. During these exercises, simple, large, school figures should be used. Try to avoid sharp turns, or riding deeply into the corners; and when changing the rein do so *out* of the circle or across the diagonals. Use free, fluid, forward, *working* gaits. It is essential not to begin with any suppling or collecting until the horse is well warmed up.

With horses of any and every level, it is sound practice to start each session with a few minutes of walk on the loose rein 'on the buckle'. This inspires confidence and relaxation in the horse, particularly in very sensitive or nervous ones (those which are prone to shying), while also serving the rider as a moment to settle down physically, and to prepare mentally for the work to come.

After some minutes of rising trot, bending the horse slightly left and right at the standstill (be sure to use the appropriate seat and leg attitudes) serves to further supple the poll and jaw, and more importantly, it teaches both horse and rider that the inside rein is used only to help bend the horse. *It is not to be used to 'steer' – to pull the creature about like a cart-horse.* Do this bending exercise slowly and deliberately and *sparingly* at the halt. One can practise this a bit more, and with less risk, at the walk or trot. However, take at least five or six strides to change the bend from one side to the other, and then maintain that new bend for five or six strides before re-bending in the opposite direction once again. *To be avoided is the quick back-and-forth bending of the neck.* This causes an incorrect 'slackness' instead of true suppleness, and lessens the quality of the

---

[1] Work the youngsters no more than three to four days a week, during their first four to six months of training. Give them plenty of time to play. They learn remarkably well when **we** learn how to hurry up slowly.

Barty. 'Walk on the loose rein' before any work has been done.

gaits. If a horse is difficult to bend, it is simply not yet balanced, and is not going freely forward in front of the rider.

Leg-yielding and turns on the forehand

These exercises must be practised sparingly. If not used carefully they can cause looseness and 'fish-tailing' of the hindquarters instead of obedience and engagement. Leg-yielding is a coarse, overt exercise. It has little gymnastic value. Nevertheless, it can be used to advantage in the early training of the horse to teach it responsiveness to leg pressure (important), or for limbering it up during the warm-up. It is also very beneficial to the student, because it effectively teaches how to coordinate the symphony of aids: in particular it helps to clarify the concept of bringing the horse up to the outside aids, and how to receive it there with the outside leg and rein. *When properly used*, the exercise can also assist the rider in freeing the horse from hanging on the reins; but this only has value when a good conversion can be made to bright, forward-working gaits *immediately* afterward – alternating, back and forth for a few minutes, between five or six steps of leg-yielding and forward gaits on single-track work. When incorrectly or over-used, however, its effects can be ruinous. Excessive use robs the horse of its forward urge, and can result in poor quality, broken gaits. The moment the horse responds willingly and lightly *for a few steps*, the exercise should be terminated.

The most common forms of leg-yielding are:

(a) from the quarter line to the wall;
(b) along the long wall of the school, either with the horse's nose pointing towards the wall, or pointing into the school;
(c) the most challenging form, leg-yielding on a volte, with the horse's nose pointing into the circle.

Important points for leg-yielding and turns on the forehand:

— *Before* asking the horse to step sideways, it is essential that it is *soft* to the inside rein.[2]
— Have a *very slight* bend towards the leg you wish to yield away from.
— Once the horse is soft to the inside rein one must then have absolutely *equal* pressure on both reins: **DO NOT PULL ON THE INSIDE REIN** to get the horse to yield. It must yield because of the leg pressure only. **Note:** the exercise is called '**LEG**-*yielding*', not '*rein-pulling*'!
— *Diagonal* aiding *initiates* the turn on the forehand. It also affects the amount of angle for the leg-yield: increase the pressure of the yielding leg (active if necessary) and *think* of its diagonal partner, the outside rein. With the exception of when a half-halt is necessary, the outside rein should not be used actively, but be sure to 'have' it and receive the horse with it (carefully guarding the alignment and unity of the horse's body, and preventing the escape of the outside shoulder), as the yielding leg establishes the angle at which the horse is to yield.

---

[2] This does not imply overbending the neck, it means only that the horse should not be against the inside rein.

— Once the desired angle has been achieved (relative to the line on which we are riding), then the *unilateral* aiding takes over to effect the sideways movement. *Without in any way altering the bend* we may, if necessary, give small 'feels' on the rein which is on the same side as the yielding leg, just to remind the horse to stay soft to it during the leg-yielding; but it is essential that the actual yielding of the horse's body comes from the leg itself.

— At leg-yielding, have not more than a 45 degree angle to the direction of travel.

— Sit stretched and square: do not collapse in the hips.

— Leave the legs long. Do not draw up the leg from which the horse is to yield.

— During *early* attempts at turns on the forehand, stop and wait after each step (neutralize, relax, and give the horse praise); do not let the horse rush around. Once competence has been gained, the entire turn can be made smoothly without stopping between steps.

050 What is the Difference Between Leg-yielding and Shoulder-in?

In leg-yielding the rider pushes the hindquarters off to the *outside* of the path taken by the forehand – **the *forehand* stays on the intended, chosen path**. The horse pivots around the inside[3] shoulder. The exercise is initiated as a turn on the forehand while in forward motion. Both front and hind legs cross over. There is only a slight bend through the horse. Its uses and value have been described above.

In shoulder-in the rider **RIDES** the forehand to the *inside* of the path taken by the hindquarters – **the *hindquarters* stay on the intended, chosen path**. The exercise is started by riding the first part of the volte. The horse pivots around the hindquarters. This is

---

[3] The 'inside' is the side towards which we wish to bend the horse.

central to correct gymnastic training, being wholly harmonious with such engaging exercises as turns on the haunches and travers. In shoulder-in, only the front legs cross over. The inside hind leg travels under the horse and directly toward the outside shoulder, and travels closely past the outside hind leg. There must be a clear bend through the horse's body.

051 Elaboration on the Suppling Exercises (047: 2)

The suppling exercises are used to establish the horse more solidly on the aids; increasing the elasticity in the horse's back; gaining control over the hindquarters, and therefore the balance; improving the unity between horse and rider. True suppleness is inseparable from a solid forward impulse from the hindquarters and from the resulting independent balance.

Suppling is best achieved through using the full range of school figures, with emphasis on 'bending in forwardness' of the horse, and making frequent changes of rein.[4] Work on circles is the first stage in moving the horse's centre of balance further back by increasing the load on one hind leg at a time (the inside one). The riding of transitions is particularly beneficial to suppling and balancing the horse, helping it to become energetically independent under the saddle. Lengthening and shortening of the strides helps to ignite the forward urge and also to confirm the dynamic balance which, in turn, prepares the horse for collection. The shoulder-in exercise is a helpful aid to achieving better degrees of bending in the horse's body.

The halt and rein-back help to engage both hind legs simultaneously, as do turns on the haunches, which further improve responsiveness to weight and leg aids. These turns are best done from the trot: trot-halt-turn-on-haunches-and-trot-on again, all in one smooth motion. Do not linger at the halt for more than a moment; however, do not rush through the turn itself.

When executing **turns on the haunches**, heed the following points:

[4] Keep in mind the important guideline regarding the 'changing of the bend' in section 049, third paragraph!!

(a) Keep the true forward intention (light, allowing hands).
(b) Do not pull the horse around with the inside rein. The inside leg and seat bone (increased weight), and the outside rein (and leg) are the most important aids by far.
(c) Keep each hand on its own side of the neck.
(d) Sit square; do not collapse in the hips.
(e) The correct sequence of walk steps must be maintained (051).

The practical value of all exercises is only realized if each rider, through methodical experimentation, discovers to which combination of loosening and suppling exercises their own horse responds most favourably. The immediate goal being that the horse puts its body entirely at the rider's disposal in as short a time as possible – 'the blank cheque state'.[5]

The practical aims in suppling the horse are, that the horse:

(a) Moves freely forward.
(b) Carries the rider equally well under both seat bones.
(c) Does not lean on one rein. Bends willingly to either side.
(d) Does not lean on, or bulge against, one of the rider's legs; readily yields to leg pressure.

The feeling of working a horse correctly is described in section 068.

052 An Introduction to the Three Basic Gaits

Correct work produces gaits which take on an appearance of elastic ease. There is a clear roundness, a ground-covering springiness and fluidity in all movement. Harmonious effortlessness, born out of balanced, energetic forwardness, are the chief hallmarks. The rider's seat is drawn forward harmoniously with the movement, borne quietly upon the supple, carrying back. There is no hint of bumping or bouncing on the saddle. If the gaits are to be considered correct by Classical standards, they must demonstrate absolute purity of

---

[5] Concept in quotes, Waldemar Seunig, from his book *Horsemanship*.

footfall, and be constant in rhythm regardless of the degree of extension or collection.

053 Work at the Walk

Definition: (a) The walk has **steps**.
            (b) It is a four-beat motion.
            (c) There is no moment of suspension.

Sequence: 1) Right hind, 2) Right front, 3) Left hind, 4) Left front.

The sequence of steps at the walk must comprise a distinct four beats, with an even, unhesitating rhythm. We must take care to keep purposeful forwardness at the walk; it is the least impulsive gait, and is therefore the most difficult in which to keep an adequate forward urge. Some essential qualities of a good walk are that it is **deliberate, languid,**[6] **fluid**, and when sufficiently advanced to do collected work, **majestic**.

Despite the challenge of maintaining adequate forward energy, the walk can be advantageously used by the student in learning how to administer the aids without being unnecessarily tossed about. It is also beneficial to practise some new exercises at the walk with young horses before the work is requested in the higher gaits. Finally, it can be a real tonic for the retrieval of spoiled horses.

A point to be strictly observed is to ride young horses at the walk on the long (or loose) rein only, until about the second year of training. The youngster must first be adequately forward-going and balanced, and demonstrate a steadiness in being 'on the aids' at the trot through simple figures and transitions, before it should be put 'on the aids' at the walk. The quality of all the gaits can be permanently ruined if the horse is prematurely put on the aids at the walk. (Artificial head carriage, improper use of the back, poor development of balance and self-carriage, and pacing can be some of the undesirable consequences.)

---

[6] By this is meant 'a slow ease', or 'strolling' quality ... not lazy, and yet void of any quickness or hectic qualities.

Modes of the walk

Extended: Hind foot steps well beyond front print.

Ordinary: Hind foot steps into or just beyond front print.

Collected: Hind foot steps short of front print; the motion is higher, rounder and more active.

054 Value of 'Walk on the Loose Rein' Within a Working Session

Besides the obvious value as a moment of rest for both horse and rider, the walk on the loose rein ('on the buckle') serves to *renaturalize* the horse, which may have become uncomfortable, tense

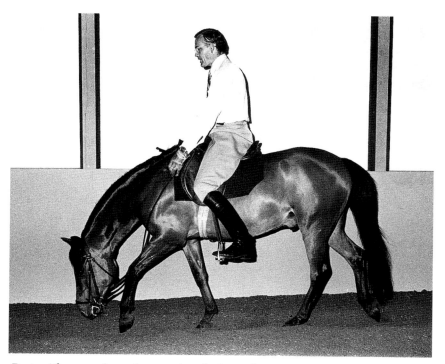

Barty. After some loosening exercises the horse drapes itself from relaxation. The horse stretches itself readily as the rider yields with the hands while driving. This attitude should be assumed any time 'walk on the loose rein' is ridden within a working session.

or resistant. It is also a helpful solution for those moments when our blood boils through frustration; the walk on the loose rein can give us a clean slate after a period of cooling-off. After walking on the loose rein for a few minutes, we should take note of the smoother motion and the longer, easier stepping. When taking up the contact once again, care should be taken to preserve this calmness and fluidity. (It is helpful, whilst taking up the rein, to *pretend* that we are still on the buckle!)

While letting the reins out through the fingers, always drive the horse into lengthening its neck forward and downward. The horse should gradually lengthen itself, as opposed to jerking the reins from the rider's hands. Should the horse jerk hard, do not fight it directly with a hard, resistant hand; instead, keep the wrist, elbow, and shoulder relaxed and by elastically and neutrally 'shock–absorbing' the jerking, give the horse nothing to fight against, and just drive a bit more. One could also place the hands *nonchalantly* on the withers or on the saddle; horses soon stop jerking when they realize they are not getting any reaction out of us, and that they are only pulling on themselves.

When riding on the loose rein, the horse must be kept moving freely forward; think of the 'flow'. '*The horse should walk as though it were going to its feed trough!*'[7]

055 Work at the Trot

Definition: (a) The trot has **strides**.
            (b) It is a two-beat motion.
            (c) There is a moment of suspension after each stride.
            (d) The presence of *diagonal unison* is of utmost importance. This means that, within the motion of any diagonal pair of legs, both legs must leave the ground (or alight on the ground again) at exactly the same moment. If the diagonal legs are not unified, an incorrect 3- or 4-beat motion results. See illustrations on page 141.

[7] Quote from Mr. Fritz Weiss, former student of Richard Wätjen.

Sequence: Diagonal pairs of legs move alternately. There is a moment of suspension (no feet touching the ground for an instant) after (between) each stride.

The bulk of riding should be carried out at the trot. It is the schooling gait for both horse and rider. The work at both the walk and canter will usually progress favourably only once the trot work becomes mature. The trot is more impulsive than the walk. It is the best gait for teaching the horse to balance itself, first on the longe, later under the rider; learning to respond to the activating aids, becoming supple and using its back and hindquarters; and above all, learning to stretch for the rider's hands, which is the foundation for all correct work.

The rider's seat and position will only develop correctly after much work at the sitting trot without stirrups, including being longed.[8] Generally, once the rider has developed a good seat at the trot, then sitting well to the walk or canter poses few problems.

Modes of the trot
Extended: Hind foot can step as much as 36in (90cm) or more beyond the front print.
Medium: An energetic long trot, showing much knee and hock action. The hind foot steps well beyond the front print.
Ordinary: (Working) Hind foot steps into or just beyond the front print.
Collected: Hind foot steps short of the front print. Croup lowered, a higher, rounder, very energetic motion. The rhythm remains even, however, and the motion is neither hovering, hectic nor tense.

056 Work at the Canter

Definition: (a) The canter has **jumps**.
            (b) It is a three–beat motion.

---

[8] But see 066, regarding use of young horses for longeing.

(c) There is a moment of suspension after the third beat.

(d) The horse is on the correct lead when the inside front leg is leading (unless counter-canter is requested).

Sequence: 1) Outside hind foot.

2) A diagonal pair of legs move in unison (inside hind foot, outside front foot).

3) Inside front foot; and then the moment of suspension.

By its very nature – a series of jumps – the canter is the most impulsive gait. Nonetheless, special care must be focused on maintaining the true forward urge and balance. It is a common mistake to slow the rhythm down, or worse yet, to attempt to collect the gait through the active use of the reins only (the backward-working hand). The horse invariably falls on the forehand, and through a combination of inactivity and tensions, the gait breaks apart: the diagonal pair of legs (second phase) no longer move simultaneously, and an incorrect four-beat motion results.

Counter-canter

At the counter-canter the horse leads with its outside front leg (e.g., the right front leg leads while riding on the left rein in the school.) The horse should always be bent in the direction of the leading leg. Counter-canter is both a collecting exercise, excellent for suppling, and a preparatory exercise for flying changes of lead.

Disunited or cross-canter

This occurs when the horse switches its lead behind (or in front) only. For example, the forehand leads right and the hindquarter leads left, or vice versa. This usually happens because the rider's seat is tense or unquiet, or the outside leg is not held clearly back (supporting the quarters), or because of imbalance or tensions in the horse.

Note: During any canter work we must keep the horse truly straight. Most horses tend to evade the honest loading of the inside hind leg by bringing the quarters toward the inside; it is a very common occurrence. For sufficiently advanced riders, it is helpful to ride the horse in a *slight* shoulder-fore position as a correction for the 'croup-in syndrome'.

Modes of the canter

Extended: Horse gains much ground at each stride; it must still be a three-beat motion.

Medium: A strong, impulsive canter, not fully extended.

Ordinary: (Working) The bulk of canter work should be executed in this mode. The length of stride should be a bit stronger than the horse might offer naturally.

Collected: The jumps are shorter and higher; not much ground is gained; the croup is well-lowered and engaged. It must be a fluid, springy three-beat motion, not tense or choppy.

057 The Canter Aid

The horse must be well prepared, and responsive especially to the bending aids; that is, it must be supple, and independently balanced under the rider.

— Horse clearly bent around the inside leg; soft and accepting on *both* reins.

— Rider's inside leg in the normal position near the girth; outside leg well back.[9]

— Rider sits relaxed, with a nicely stretched body position, and inside seat bone slightly forward.

— The *outside* leg (passively applied) says, 'AND!', then the *inside* seat bone, applying greater weight and forward-urging pressure, says, 'can–TER'! If the horse doesn't react crisply to

[9] Keep weight through the lowered outside heel, and stretch it towards the horse's outside hind foot (031).

the inside seat bone alone, the inside leg may give an *active* nudge at the same time, and even this may be further reinforced with a tap from the stick, if necessary. The outside leg gives the same pressure but is held passively. A half-halt is given just before the aid to canter-on. This balances the horse and frees it from the hand. We must clearly lighten the hands, especially the inside rein, at the canter strike-off.

— To maintain the canter, the aid to 'canter-on' is repeated at each stride, more or less. This might be just 'the subtlest of hints' from the inside seat bone only,[10] or a fairly loud aid with the 'full orchestra', as the moment requires.

Be careful not to force or surprise the horse with the canter aid, as tensions and rushing will result. With young horses it is best to strike-off to the canter from the trot, using the corner of the school to help juggle-up the correct lead. One may need to reinforce the canter aid with the stick (either at the horse's inside shoulder, or behind the rider's outside leg), until the horse becomes familiar with the signal from seat (weight aid) and leg alone. One should not strike-off to the canter from the walk until well into the second year of training; the horse should first be well established in walk 'on the aids'.

It is a common mistake to force the horse back into the canter immediately after it has fallen from the canter into an unbalanced, rushing trot. When this happens, the rider should instead always take time to bring the horse back down quietly into a good, rhythmic, balanced and relaxed trot before striking-off into canter once again. With more advanced horses one should make the transition down to the walk before commencing the canter again; this improves the balance, suppleness and use of the back, and the engagement of the hindquarters.

Should the horse strike-off on the wrong lead, or cross-canter, we mustn't get rough with it, snatching it back sharply to the trot or walk. Instead, we can use this mistake to our advantage. Only a fool

---

[10] We talk about the seat bone, but this is inseparable from suitable upper body attitudes. See Chapter II, and 021–023, 060.

rejects a happy accident! We can ride the counter-canter for a few moments *deliberately*; it will help to supple the horse. Then patiently bring it through the downward transition, and after a few moments of better preparation try the correct lead again. Only adequate preparation (suppling, balancing) will produce the correct lead consistently.[11]

058 Transitions

All transitions, including the lengthening and shortening of the stride within the gaits, going from gait to gait, and making half-halts at any time, are occasions in which the rider must reconfirm the horse's balance by assuring adequate forward desire. Transitions must be decisive, fluid, and forward in nature. They should give the work an appearance of seamlessness.

By and large, a transition, or the respective, resulting gait will be only as good as the work in the previous gait.

'Single' transitions are a simple progression, for example: halt to walk, walk to trot, and trot to canter. 'Double' or 'triple' transitions (also called 'direct') entail skipping interim gaits, for example: halt to trot, or walk to canter, or canter to halt, etc. Use only the 'single' transitions (especially downward) for young horses.

059 The Halt

An experienced rider on a well-suppled horse can demonstrate halts, half-halts and rein-back with a feather-light contact. In a correct halt the horse should come to stand squarely and quietly on all four legs. An unsquare halt is a sign that the horse was not truly supple, and that it was not stepping up to both sides of the bit evenly before the halt was executed.

A truly correct halt can only be executed on a horse which is

---

[11] This presupposes, of course, that the rider's seat and aids are correct. Most canter errors can be directly traced to false seat influences.

Atlantis. The halt. The horse is held 'at the aids' with seat and legs; the hand remains passive.

sufficiently active, supple, and well on the aids (balanced), whereby the 'circuit' is complete (041). Adequate forward desire and the resultant even reaching for both reins are indispensable to obtaining a good halt. We must *ride* the horse (passively) up to a restraining (sustaining) hand. The hand must filter the forward energy in a soft, elastic way. This is strictly an *attitude* of the hand, and does not constitute a pulling in any sense of the word. Furthermore, the hand should not become hard and fixed. This can lock up the horse's back, kill the impulsion and throw the horse heavily onto the forehand. Several small, active half-halts may be given during the halting procedure if the horse doesn't as yet react well to the passive aids from the seat/position. While halting or performing a half-halt, we must be well let down, relaxed on the 'triangle', with head up and a well stretched position. Note particularly the essential position indicators given in 009, with regard to the 'front line'; the 'completion of the circuit' (041); and the importance of the head position (014, 022).

When correctly executed, the halt (and rein-back) can be an effective key to the increased loading of the hindquarters. It can improve the balance, independence, and general obedience of the horse.

060 The Half-halt

The half-halt is first and foremost a balancing tool. It is the main key to forging harmony between horse and rider. This is so because only when the horse is independently balanced does it begin to carry and complete, or 'fill', the seat and leg so that the rider can find a comfortable place to sit (50 per cent of the seat is made up by the horse!). The half-halt is also the single most important avenue to liberating the horse's powers. Through this freedom, founded on independent balance (self-carriage) true suppleness can be developed; which in turn enables the horse's energy to travel *unimpeded* through its whole body.

Because it revitalizes and rebalances the horse, the half-halt has the excellent preparatory function of setting the horse up in *balanced readiness* before corners, before changing the bend, and before all transitions. The half-halt, therefore, assists the rider to re-animate the horse, gaining a brighter, more vigorous stepping, without changing the rhythm while in motion, and prevents the horse from taking possession of the hand (leaning).

For the half-halt to be correct and effective, the horse must be responsive to the forward-driving aids: that is, it must be 'driveable'. '*Every half-halt implies the need for greater driving* [animating]'.[12] Only once the horse has responded to the driving influences from the seat/position and legs, by filling the reins with forward energy, should the hand offer a momentary sustaining – '***close*-open**' – (for no more than a stride), and then allow the horse freely forward again. The driving aid predominates and momentarily outlasts the

---

[12] Egon von Neindorff.

rein influence. After the half-halt, depending on the circumstances, the hands can either assume only an *attitude* of allowing (without actually giving forward measurably), or they can be given forward measurably (both hands equally) towards the horse's mouth; taking care, however, neither to lose the contact, nor to let the horse come off the aids and lose its self-carriage, by over-giving. The *active* driving aids must stop when the horse has responded to them, while the seat remains nicely forward in the saddle (the *maintaining* seat 022: 2), and the relaxed calves lightly and passively hug the horse's sides. Just the presence of the seat and legs in this fashion prevents the newly-gained balance from creeping out from underneath the seat.

If the half-halt succeeds, the horse will respond to the temporary 'sustaining' effect of the reins by gathering itself up under the rider's centre of balance, 'filling' the seat, and becoming lighter on the contact. Should the half-halt not succeed, then tune the horse once again to the driving aids, and try again. The half-halt may be repeated as frequently as is necessary to achieve the desired animating/balancing results.

To half-halt as often as necessary does not mean that we should fiddle endlessly and aimlessly with the hand; that only makes the mouth insensitive, as a result of which ever more and stronger aids need to be given to achieve any effects. The half-halts should only be used deliberately, *when necessary*, not just for good measure. To be of value, *each* half-halt must go through the entire cycle: drive – receive – become lighter again. It is important to realize that it is **not** the active 'rein effect' on the outside rein, in and of itself, that gets the horse's head to come into place … rather it is the balance achieved through a momentary 'capturing of the animation' that causes the desired head carriage. To further underscore this point, when the horse is adequately prepared (is obedient to the seat and legs, is suppled and willing to bend, and correctly 'on the aids'), the half-halt can be executed *without* an active hand at all, using the driving aid from the seat and leg, and receiving that energy with a *momentary and passive* sustaining attitude in the hand (which is inseparable and indistinguishable from the attitude which is taken up in our body position). See 009, front line and 022, attitudes of the seat.

Be sure to avoid the following common pitfalls:

(a) Getting tied up with the hands by continuously hanging on the reins when the half-halt does not succeed – always keep the hands relaxed, free, independent.
(b) Half-halting with the hand alone, without it being well supported in the seat/position (front line) and legs.
(c) Letting the half-halt degenerate into a crass jerking on the reins; or half-halting actively with both reins simultaneously.

In learning how to perform the half-halt it can be helpful to begin by riding some single transitions, walk–halt, halt–walk; or walk–trot, trot–walk. When the horse begins to expect us to make more transitions, we then need only *think* of making the downward transition and the horse will readily react. For example, at the walk the rider should think of coming to the halt, but just before the horse actually halts, the rider says to the horse 'I've changed my mind, let's continue to walk'. One could do likewise between the walk and the trot, suspending the horse between the 'halting' idea, and the 'trotting-on' idea. This is, of course, a very exaggerated exercise, and it should only be used temporarily. The rider should learn to perform half-halts in a much more subtle way, so that the observer cannot see the horse drastically changing its pace. Ideally, the horse should stay in the same rhythm, and the observer should see only a better quality of forwardness, and an overall improvement in the horse's balance.

Though good seat and position attitudes are central to the success of all riding, there is probably no place where this shows up more clearly than during the halt and half-halt. We must be well let down, *resting* on our 'triangle', and be entirely free of tensions, especially in our hip joints, shoulders, and arms (for details see Chapter II.)

What do we do with the seat and position?
POSITION:
— *Vertical upper body*; head up; carry book on head.
— *Long, open front line*, stomach leading … (the billowing, forward-drawing sail).

— *Bent, relaxed, heavy elbows.*
— Hips leading, and angle of 'pelvic tilt' as needed.[13]

ATTITUDES:
— Well stretched from heel to head.
— During the half-halt, turn the hip joints to water.
— Push forward **from the lower back** (the top of the pelvis) *without hollowing the lower back*; this is the 'source' of the forward energy. Concurrently, *draw* forward with the front line (navel, solar plexus leading).
— Breathe in, expanding the diaphragm down into the hips.
— Softly broaden the hips.
— Softly broaden the shoulders.
(Take on these above *attitudes* as the hand *temporarily* closes)

What do we do with the hands?
POSITION:
— Hand on the line from the elbow to the horse's mouth.
— Hands vertical.

ATTITUDES:
— 'Hold' or 'confirm' or 'have' the inside rein passively.[14]
— Half-halt (**'*close*–open'**) actively on the outside rein; **or** just *passively sustain* with both reins if an active half-halt is unnecessary.
— Soften *both* reins equally, *and immediately* after the half-halt. (*Yield* them slightly forward towards the horse's mouth.)

Also remember, either active hand, or active leg (with engaged seat); do not use both *actively* at the same time. One may, for example, drive with an engaged seat and passive hugging legs as the hand (outside rein) half-halts actively; or conversely, one may resist (sustain) elastically and passively with the reins as the seat

---

[13] Without raising the pubic bone off the saddle; without shortening the front line; and without leaning back.
[14] This stabilizes the neck, keeping it from changing (looking out) when the active half-halt is given on the outside rein.

engages and the inside leg drives actively.

— The rider's driving aids say, 'Come on, liven up!' (Clearly stretched, open front line, and look to the horizon.)
— *Then* the hand says, 'But stay in rhythm.'[15] (Then yields.)
— DRIVE ... RECEIVE ... BECOME LIGHTER AGAIN ... (then drive ... while giving with the hand).

061 The Rein-back

The rein-back originates from the driving aids. In this case, however, the seat is lightened by bringing the upper body *slightly* forward from the waist (keep the 'triangle' on the saddle). This opens the back door, and allows the horse to go backward.

The rider's legs say, 'Move'. All the hands say is 'Not forward'.

The hand is strictly *not* to pull the horse backward, though small alternating 'feels' may be given on the reins in time with the stepping of each corresponding hind foot. (This is a very subtle influence, and has nothing to do with *sawing* on the horse's mouth, or pulling back!)

To stop the rein-back, we begin by closing the back door by sitting upright again, then press the seat bones into the front of the saddle and emphasize the legs, while clearly yielding with the hands (do not lose the contact, nor throw away the 'carriage' of the horse.)

The correct rein-back is constituted in an absolutely pure diagonal stepping: a two-beat motion, without a moment of suspension. If the horse has a resistant back, or if the rider's hand pulls back actively, an incorrect four-beat motion results. The horse's legs must be picked up clearly. Dragging feet are a sign of incorrect work; characteristics of resistance or tension.

To use more than 5–6 steps of rein-back at any one time would constitute a punishment. Making any more than ten steps

---

[15] ... 'Stay under me' ... 'Gather under me'.

Barty. Rein-back. Here the horse is showing difficulties in its back, indicated by the relatively open position of the head/neck, and the stiffness in its front legs, which appear to be stuck to the ground. Its non-yielding attitude is also mirrored in its unhappy facial expression.

backward becomes unacceptable, because it endangers the tendons and joints which can suffer damage from such senseless practice.

Both the halt and rein-back must be executed with a straight horse; any lateral evasions must be carefully prevented (using diagonal aids).[16]

---

[16] Using the leg on the side of the evading croup, in conjunction with the rein on the opposite side.

Atlantis. Rein-back. Here is a more advanced horse in exactly the same rein-back phase as the opposite photo. Showing a good attitude psychologically, and a correct yielding attitude of the neck (back). The rider is just in the process of erecting the upper body and bracing the back to come to the halt. Comparatively, the photo opposite shows clearly the 'unloading' of the horse's back (rider leaning forward) during the actual process of reining-back. In both photographs a correct diagonal stepping is illustrated.

062 A Definition of Two-track Work

Any work which is not ridden straight (that is, on a single track, 035) is referred to as two-track work. This is irrespective of whether the horse's legs make three or four separate tracks. The issue is that the forehand and hindquarters each travel on their own separate paths. The moment we *deliberately* ride with the hind legs *outside* the path

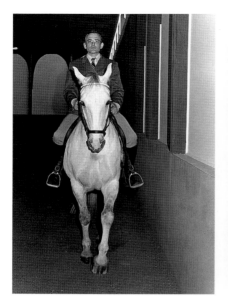

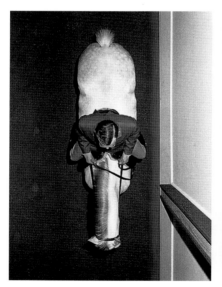
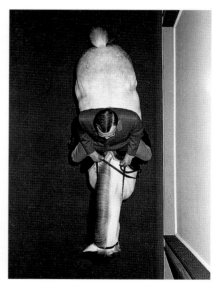

Work on the straight line(065). From above, the rider's hips and shoulders are exactly square, sitting over the centre of the horse. When observing the horse from the front, one should see only TWO legs.

Position Right. It should be noted that in all these photos, the horse travels parallel to the school walls.

taken by the front legs, it can be technically considered two-track work.

Correct two-track work should not be confounded with uncontrolled crookedness caused either by the rider's uneven position or aiding, or by the horse's natural one-sidedness. It is not recommended for the beginner to practise any two-track work (the sparing use of turns on the forehand and leg-yielding excepted) until very thoroughly acquainted with riding the horse 'on the aids' on all simple school figures, in the three basic gaits, riding these on a single track (029).

It is beyond the scope of this brief text to engage in a detailed study of the value of all two-track work. However, the most significant foundation, which is shoulder-in, will be fully described. Basically, two-track work should not be used as an end in itself. There is nothing particularly noteworthy about being able to make a horse go sideways. Though it is requested in many dressage tests to demonstrate the rider's control, it is crucial to understand that any and all exercises we do should be aimed at one goal only: the improvement of the quality, purity and balance of the three basic gaits *in single-track work!*

Two-track work can be validly implemented by experienced riders to further the suppleness of the back and hindquarters, and to improve the general responsiveness, malleability and balance of the horse. Under the guidance of a competent instructor, two-track work can also be a helpful learning tool for sufficiently advanced students.

063 Shoulder-in

Of what value is the shoulder-in exercise?
(a) It helps to further the bend at the horse's rib-cage, which in turn is essential to achieving greater bending of the three major joints of the hind legs. This enables the hindquarters to lower.
(b) It helps the rider to further supple the stiff side of the horse, and therefore contributes to straightness, and to the horse's even reaching into both reins.

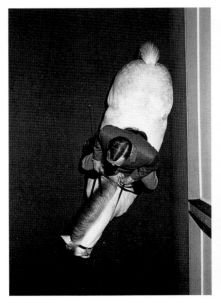

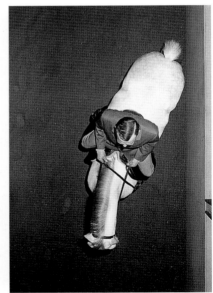

Shoulder-in right. This represents the SECOND POSITION. (See footnote 17)

Renvers. (The reverse exercise to travers.)

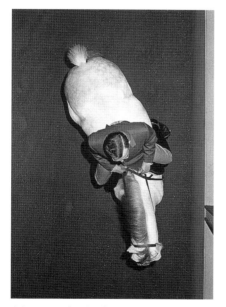

Travers right. (When practised across the diagonal of the school it is called HALF-PASS).

Leg-yielding, away from the left leg. (Can also be practised with the horse facing toward the inside of the school – 049).

The First Position. This is a good example of 'head tipping' (ears not on the same level). The horse is not stepping evenly into both reins (see 038e, p65).

(c) It helps to put the horse more clearly onto the inside leg and outside rein.

(d) It helps to improve the horse's balance, and the suppleness of the hindquarters. It can therefore be used as a collecting exercise.

(e) It is the basic preparatory exercise for all other two-track (lateral) work in all three gaits. Every step of half-pass and turns on the haunches, for example, should have the 'seed' of shoulder-in wholly entrenched within it.

Note: These positive effects from shoulder-in can only be gained if the horse has first been well prepared and put correctly 'on the aids' in single-track work.

Technical requirements

(A description of the full shoulder-in, or second position).[17]

(a) The exercise is ridden on *three* tracks. The outside hind foot makes one track; the inside hind foot follows exactly in the path of the outside front foot, making the second track; last, the inside front foot makes the third track.

(b) The horse must be bent through its whole body, with as much bend as possible in the body. Take care, however, that there is not too much bend in the neck; especially not at its base.[18]

(c) The hindquarter travels straight along the wall. Only the forehand is brought slightly over to the inside of the school.

064 Practical Implementation of Two-track Work

(a) For any two-track work it is essential that the horse goes more forward than sideways.

---

[17] THE FIRST POSITION, or shoulder-fore, is a preparatory exercise for shoulder-in. It is basically the same exercise as the second position but the horse does not come off the wall quite so far. In the 'first' position the inside hind leg travels in a path that runs exactly between both front legs. Its aim is to achieve a sound bend, and to cause the hind legs to travel closer together, which is the basis for improving balance and control in general.

18 See just a glimpse of the inside eye and nostril rim. It is a common fault to overbend the neck beyond that point.

(b) The horse must be 'on the aids' (active and balanced), before the exercise is attempted.

(c) Care must be taken to remain sitting square in the saddle. Do not collapse in the hips.

(d) Start the exercise after the second corner of the short side of the school, or from a volte. Do not wrestle the horse into a shoulder-in position with the reins, rather, *ride* the forehand off the wall, as though you want to begin a volte. As the forehand starts to come off the wall, indicate to the horse that it should go along the wall at the desired angle by giving a half-halt, then emphasize the inside seat bone/leg and feel the outside rein (equal weight in both reins anyway!) The inside leg attends to the forward motion.

(e) It is extremely important that the rider's outside leg is well on the horse. Without its presence the forward energy from the inside leg does not arrive at the bridle, and thus the horse will lose its energy and balance. One could say that the passive outside leg *converts* the energy, generated by the active inside leg, into balance and forwardness by directing it towards the bit. This holds true for turns on the forehand, leg-yielding, and shoulder-in. (See 020, 'outside leg'!).[19]

(f) As with all two-track work, shoulder-in must be practised with great discretion. The bulk of all work should be carried out on a single track. The horse's gaits, especially the forward urge, suffer adversely when two-track work is practised incorrectly or superfluously.

(g) If a problem arises (crookedness; resistance or constrained forward motion; unlevel gaits), the horse must be corrected by better balancing and suppling in single-track work. Go immediately onto a large circle, and ride the horse freely forward in working gaits until the gaits become pure and active once more.

[19] Because the horse only seems to respond in a 'forward manner' when the outside leg is properly on the horse, this *passive* function of the outside leg (which 'shunts' the energy towards the bridle) can easily be misconstrued as being the 'active' driving aid. But no, indeed, only the inside leg should give the *active* driving impulse to the horse. As we know, both legs should have the same pressure during driving. We must constantly sandwich the horse between both legs equally – this is doubly important during two-track work.

065 Importance of Riding on 'Straight Lines': Single-track Work

Bending exercises are used to supple the horse, in order to be able to straighten it (035). It is therefore essential that plenty of work on ruler-straight lines also be ridden; on the second (inside) track, across diagonals, and on the centre line (away from school walls) – this is particularly important for young horses.

While riding on straight lines, the rider must sit exactly square in the saddle, with both legs in the same position. The outside leg is **not** brought back on straight lines, unless momentary correcting aids need to be given; or when riding with a bend, or in 'position' (see overhead photographs pages 106–7).

066 Of What Value is the Riding of School Figures?

The accurate riding of school figures, paying close attention to the purity of their form, size and location, gives us an essential purpose whereby we can assess our riding and evaluate where our control is lacking. It is an essential part of our leadership, and when we are consistent, persistent and insistent about maintaining the school figures of our choice, most horses immediately go better, even for fairly weak riders. Flitting about aimlessly, or being sloppy about the school figures, has little or no schooling value for either horse or rider. Furthermore, when the figures are ridden 'Calm, Forward, and Straight' (035) they become a valuable tool in helping students initially put their horses 'on the aids' correctly.

067 School Figures

The school figures should be practised equally on both reins in order to exercise and develop the complete muscle structure, balance, and ambidexterity of the horse. While the basic school figures are shown in the accompanying diagrams, below are some further points of interest.

SCHOOL/ARENA SIZE 40x20m (132x66ft) SCHOOL/ARENA SIZE 40x20m (132x66ft)

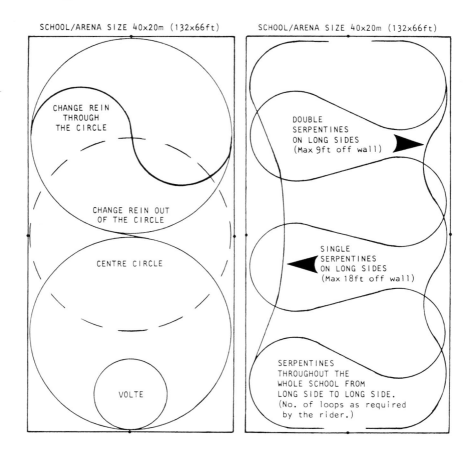

CHANGE REIN
THROUGH
THE CIRCLE

CHANGE REIN OUT
OF THE CIRCLE

CENTRE CIRCLE

VOLTE

DOUBLE
SERPENTINES
ON LONG SIDES
(Max 9ft off wall)

SINGLE
SERPENTINES
ON LONG SIDES
(Max 18ft off wall)

SERPENTINES
THROUGHOUT THE
WHOLE SCHOOL FROM
LONG SIDE TO LONG SIDE.
(No. of loops as required
by the rider.)

(a) With the exception of the initial 'loosening' work, it is important to ride well into the corners of the school. Here we can learn to bend the horse around our inside leg, and ask for activity without the horse rushing away from the driving aids. Take note, however, that with unbalanced young horses, the corners should be well rounded-off, especially at the trot and canter.

    – *Remember to prepare the horse well BEFORE the corner by riding 'position', give a half-halt, then LET the horse flow through the corner (pushing both hands forward) while emphasizing the driving aids.* Essentially, a corner is 'well ridden' *before* the corner, not *in* the corner itself, when it is

112

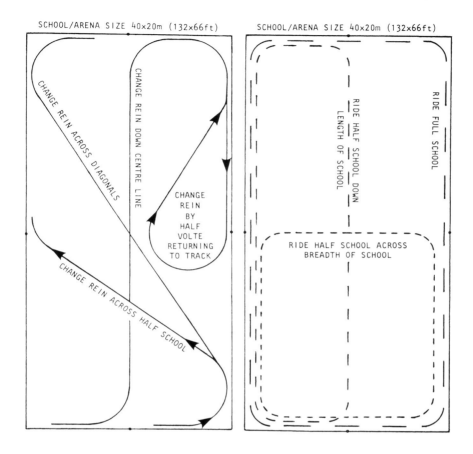

SCHOOL/ARENA SIZE 40x20m (132x66ft)

CHANGE REIN ACROSS DIAGONALS

CHANGE REIN DOWN CENTRE LINE

CHANGE REIN ACROSS HALF SCHOOL

CHANGE REIN BY HALF VOLTE RETURNING TO TRACK

SCHOOL/ARENA SIZE 40x20m (132x66ft)

RIDE HALF SCHOOL DOWN LENGTH OF SCHOOL

RIDE FULL SCHOOL

RIDE HALF SCHOOL ACROSS BREADTH OF SCHOOL

too late and only produces tensions in the horse.

(b) While riding on large circles, an excellent exercise to practise is 'circle decrease–circle increase'; making the circle smaller by gradually spiralling towards the centre (moving the horse away from the outside aids) until the circle is either 10m or volte size, then enlarging it once again to full size (by leg-yielding away from the inside leg.)

(c) Riding on the second track (6–8ft [2m] from the school walls, and parallel to the walls) is an ideal exercise to emphasize the need to contain the horse within the rider's 'river-banks' at all times (038). While practising this exercise the rider should ride diligently into the *imaginary* corners.

(d) Another productive and educational school figure is to ride squares (of various sizes), for the same reasons as point (c) above.

Reflections V

— Correct transitions are the proof of the pudding.

— Always bend the horse in the direction you are going. The only exceptions are: 1) shoulder-in; 2) leg-yielding; 3) counter-canter; 4) when *deliberately* riding 'counter-bend' in any gait.

— When riding any curved lines the horse must be bent throughout its whole body, not just at the head and neck.

— Simplicity is the strength of the exercise.

— When straightening the horse, line up the shoulders with the hindquarters, rather than trying to push the quarters over to line up with the forehand.

— It is incorrect to press the horse toward the outside of a circle or turn, or ride into a corner, by bringing the inside rein against the neck. It is a sign that the inside seat bone and/or leg is not doing its job, and that the horse is also not *on* the outside rein correctly.

— Only when we ourselves become truly ambidextrous, can we expect our horses to work equally well on both reins.

— Advanced work is only ever as good as the basics.

— Stability and balance in the horse can only be established through a resolute forward urge. This is fundamental in maintaining purity of the gaits.

— Do not work the horse more on its difficult side; work it equally on both reins. Frequent changes of rein 'brings home the bacon' faster than dogged grinding on the weaker side.

— Ultimately, a smooth performance is made up of a continuous series of minor corrections, before major problems have manifest themselves.

— The rider should always determine the exact length of

stride to be ridden, and not just go around in some ill-defined gait.

— Only the rider can give intelligent purpose to the work: *the horse needs a leader.*

— Be visionary, not reactionary ... look, and think, and *act* ahead.

Barty. Working canter right.

CHAPTER VI

General Observations

Riding must be pleasing to the eye and to the feelings.
Egon von Neindorff

Introduction

The prime task of dressage riding is to assist the horse to move more efficiently and beautifully while carrying the rider. So long as we simply 'hack' our horses around inoffensively, leaving the creatures to their own devices, we will probably neither harm nor improve the motion of the three unschooled gaits. However, the moment we wish to affect the horse's way of going this immediately becomes a complex and serious undertaking, that must be handled with careful consideration and respect. It is far easier to detract from the horse's natural integrity and beauty than to enhance them. Thus, before we can hope to improve on the basic gaits, we must acquire a reasonably good understanding of the nature of the 'raw material' with which we are working.

While learning how to influence the horse correctly, we can avoid going seriously off-track by becoming acquainted with the signals given by the horse, indicating its acceptance or rejection of our work. The next two sections outline these aspects in detail. Besides being general guidelines, these points are also good indicators for establishing parameters for the following pertinent issues:

— How much driving is suitable for the horse's state of suppleness, balance and level of training.
— What limitations to set on the level and complexity of exercises.
— When, and for how long, to do sitting trot (young horses).
— Determining the degree of collection that is acceptable for any given state of training.

If any of the 'positive' aspects fall by the wayside, and any of the 'negative' signs show their ugly head, the rider should lessen the demands on the horse: simplify the exercises or school figures; ride freer gaits; and with young horses go back to rising trot, until the horse becomes more approachable and accepting once again.

068 What are the Signs of Correct Work?

— The first sign that the horse is beginning to relax and use its muscle ring[1] correctly is that it starts to snort or 'blow'.
— Because of forwardness and balance, the horse's back becomes supple and swinging. It wells–up beneath the rider's seat and becomes easy to sit on. It carries the rider 'up and forward' with it, evenly under both seat bones.
— The horse's rib-cage fills, making it easier for the rider to keep the legs on; it allows them to hang down relaxed and stretched; the lower legs especially are effortlessly 'sucked' onto the horse's sides. This also makes it possible to ride correctly with the calves (instead of the back of the leg or heels).
— Because the horse is united, the gaits become pure;[2] they are 'rounder', more clearly cadenced, and springy. Though nicely active, they are soft, elastic, and become uncannily quiet.
— The tail is carried and swings gently with the motion.
— The horse is in front of the rider's seat and leg;[3] the forehand

---

[1] See section 035, completion of the circuit.
[2] Walk 053; trot 055; canter 056.
[3] The old standard: 'Two-thirds of the horse in front of the rider, one-third behind.'

becomes large and light because the shoulder is freed owing to a greater 'carrying' of the supple, engaged and deeply bent hindquarters.

— The horse becomes easy to keep straight. Halts are easily executed and square. Transitions are fluid and clean.

— There is a good, soft, elastic feeling in the hand; the hind legs 'pulse' in the reins.

— The horse responds well to the driving aids. Its whole body lengthens readily in answer to the driving aids; and/or the gaits lengthen when the rider's hands yield forward towards the bit. In both extensions and collection the rhythm remains even, not erratic, and the back remains continuously easy to sit on.[4]

— The horse's facial expression is quiet, peaceful, contented and accepting;[5] yet, at the same time, it is full of eagerness; its eyes sparkling with life and joy.

— As a result of its supple, animated state the horse reaches for the bit and begins to chew quietly, producing a *firm* foam on its lips. More is better.[6]

069 Points to Watch for in Incorrect Work

PROBLEM

Stiffness, unwilling to bend, hard to steer.

CAUSE[7]

Lack of forwardness and balance; lack of suppleness; tensions[8] in

---

[4] If the horse is hard to sit on, especially during extensions, tensions and improper use of the horse's back muscles are indicated.

[5] Indicated particularly by the attitude of the eyes, ears, nostrils and lips.

[6] When the saliva is too watery it is usually a sign of nervousness, which might further be characterized by a noisy, exaggerated biting at the bit. The dry mouth indicates that the horse is not stepping properly through the poll; the poll and jaw are not yet relaxed.

[7] If the horse should not appear to be performing as well as usual, the rider should keep in mind the possibility that it might not be feeling completely well. It may be suffering from slight colic, cramps, stiffness, or might simply not be in 'good form' to whatever physical or psychological reasons. The horse is not a machine!

[8] TENSIONS can be caused by a wide variety of reasons, usually, however, by the rider's own tensions, or by forcing of the horse; or the horse is not sufficiently prepared for the work being asked of it; or because of nervousness or fright. For an effective remedy see 035 through 046, and 070, 071, 072.

horse's back and neck, general resistance. Rough, dominant hands.

Rough trot and canter; hard to sit on.

Horse's back stiff, its muscles not in proper use; circuit not complete; lack of balance, activity; gaits broken apart. Stiff rider.

Too fast a rhythm, rushing.

Imbalance; nervousness, tensions, discomfort, not relaxed in back; overriding; insensitive driving; soreness.

Grinding teeth, noisy biting at the bit; mouth open; tongue hanging out; unquiet expression in eyes.

Horse unhappy, work not in harmony with its nature; experiencing pain, mental distress; lack of true forwardness; rider forcing; hard, dominant, or over-active hands.

Swishing of tail.

Mental resistance; rough aids; horse experiencing discomfort or pain, or is ticklish (caution with spurs); rider not in harmony with horse's nature; rider's leg is more dominant than the seat.

Horse heavy, boring on the hand (face often behind the vertical).

Lack of activity, balance; horse rushing; on the forehand. Heavy or dead hands; rider stiff, or *lacks independence* of seat, upper body, hands. Artificial collection, false training methods.

Crookedness.	Horse not framed and/or not supple; not reaching evenly into both reins; horse pressed together too soon into collected work; hand bottling horse up. Lameness.
Tossing of head.	Lack of balance and/or discomfort in horse's back; rider stiff, hands too dominant, unquiet or hard; lack of balance between driving and receiving aids; bridle badly adjusted; saddle fitting poorly; least likely, though possible, problems with teeth.
Forging or 'clicking' (hind foot striking sole or shoe of front foot).	Lack of honest forwardness; horse on the forehand; actively using hind legs, but its back is not in play (leg-goer). Least likely, shoeing or trimming job not suited to horse's build or way of going.
Dull, lifeless eyes, withdrawn facial expression.	The horse's natural desire and eagerness have been destroyed through the rider's (or handler's) tyranny. The horse has been robbed off its 'vote' and of its very 'horseness' ... its nature.

070 Causes of Rider-induced Tensions in the Horse

Though tension certainly can be caused by outside influences, the preponderant source of tension in the horse usually originates with the rider. The following are the most common causes; *all of these points are also strong contributors to incidents of shying:*

— our own fear or anxiety
— our own physical tension or stiffness
— our own one-sidedness or crookedness
— our lack of tactfulness
— when we make a 'big deal' about anything
— when we engage in any direct confrontation with the horse
— harsh, blunt, or insensitive use of any aids; especially the rein aids
— clutching hands or legs … 'hanging on' (for dear life)
— unfair or unreasonable use of whip or spurs
— inadvertent unbalancing of the horse, usually caused by our own imbalance, or an inappropriate, or ill-prepared, choice of school figures or exercises
— insufficiently careful preparation (each and every day again) with a sound programme of loosening and suppling exercises
— pressing the horse too quickly in its general training programme, especially forced collection: *over-facing!*

Indications of tensions in the horse

— shying: when a horse feels stressed it starts to see ghosts
— the horse becomes unsteady, unbalanced, veers and darts about abruptly
— the feeling in the reins becomes dead, hard, jolting or empty
— the gaits lose their elasticity, becoming flat, jarring, expressionless, unsteady, erratic in rhythm
— the horse's back becomes difficult to sit on: our legs can no longer hang effortlessly on the horse's sides.

071 Antidotes for Nervous, Excited, or Tense Horses

— We must melt,[9] that is, relax both mentally and physically.
— Have a soft, pliant seat. Rising trot may be advisable.

---

[9] Extra mozzarella!

— Keep the legs on, with a supple, caressing, neutral attitude.
— Have a gentle, steady, elastic contact; possibly guide the hands on the neck; or take both reins in one hand and stroke or pat the neck gently with the free hand.
— Keep the rhythm/tempo even; half-halt *judiciously*, don't hang on, keep the hands independent; always end up with a light, giving quality in the hands.
— Use simple school figures, and exercises, until the horse settles down. Walk the horse 'on the buckle', using a smaller circle for a while (or possibly a 10m figure-of-eight pattern, staying on any one rein for about 4–5 circles before changing) until the horse settles.
— *We must pay no direct attention to the horse's excited state,* concentrating instead only on our own relaxation and on the work at hand (school figure, gait, exercise).

072 Shying

Though sensitive or nervous horses are generally more likely to do so, any horse might shy at some time or other. It is simply the nature of the horse to flee from that which it perceives to be potential danger. The shying in and of itself is not a problem. Our reactions to such incidents, however, can either deftly diffuse them into boring insignificance, or cause them to become an all-pervading, deeply confirmed dilemma which constantly disrupts the work. When horses shy a lot it is usually a sign that they have little confidence in their rider (leader). Besides needing to develop a solid mental, emotional, and physical self-control, to succeed in maintaining or regaining the horse's confidence in us requires tactfulness, and deep, unflappable patience on our part. For *bold riders*, any impatience, or any forcing of the horse,[10] especially with regard to this subject, will cause things to degenerate – guaranteed! For *timid riders*, it is absolutely essential to learn to be non-reactionary, that is, to stay

---

[10] Particularly, any forcing of the horse to go to the site or object at which it is apparently shying, is most destructive.

relaxed, and not to begin to grab or clutch at the horse. Under the circumstances of shying horses need, above all, a steady, calm, confident leader. Neither the bully nor the faint-hearted soul will succeed in helping the horse regain its confidence. There are two main causes for shying:

1) The rider's attitudes or actions (for causes and solutions, see 070 and 071).
2) External incidents.

The following points give guidance for how best to diffuse the negative energy of shying:

— It is absolutely crucial that we pay no attention to the real or imagined object from which the horse is shying. Even if a bomb drops next to the riding school we should be so non-reactionary that, so far as the horse should be concerned, *the rider can't see or hear anything!*
— Do not look at, or try to find out what caused the shying; to do so makes us agree with the horse's reaction, and makes us an accomplice to it.
— Keep cool. Do not get emotionally involved. Be bored.
— Bend the horse away from the frightening object.
— Pass the 'bogyman' in a shoulder-in attitude. But think only of the shoulder-in – **not** of making the horse go 'T-H-E-R-E!!'
— *Do not force your horse to go to the place which is causing the stress.* We must ignore it totally, and concentrate instead on another school figure. That will best help the horse to begin to feel confident in our guidance, and gradually begin to go quietly and trustingly anywhere in the school once more.
— As we approach and pass by the problem spot, we must *relax the contact very deliberately and push both hands gently towards the horse's mouth.*
— Then we should quietly tune the horse to the inside leg *somewhere else* in the school with a little bit of shoulder-in, strictly avoiding making a big issue of it, especially at the site of the shying. In time, we can nonchalantly make a few

124

passes by the problem spot, making sure we very deliberately relax (specially the contact) as we *approach and pass by* it while keeping the legs on gently and passively, yet steadily.

— Praise the horse either with voice or by quietly patting the neck *after* passing the problem area. Then forget about the whole issue completely! Act as though nothing happened. Just get on with the work. The sooner we forget about it, the sooner the horse will forget about it, and settle in and begin to work normally again.

073 Which Bits Should be Used?

Most of the work in the training of either horse or rider should be done with a plain, mild snaffle bit (loose-ring, eggbutt, full-check, Fulmer). Because the snaffle is jointed in the middle, it can act unilaterally on either side of the horse's mouth: a prerequisite in helping to teach the horse initially how to yield to the bending aids (a task which must be well underscored with appropriate seat and leg attitudes). There is only one factor which determines the severity of the plain snaffle bit – the thinner the mouthpiece, the more severe the bit.

Today, the double bridle is generally used as a formality in the higher levels of dressage competitions. However, though it can be, it does not necessarily have to be part of the horse's training. **IF** a *horse is well prepared* (that is a very significant 'IF'!) the curb can make access to the bending of the hind legs somewhat easier in some cases; and can, under certain circumstances, alleviate the task in the advanced training of some particularly resistant, bullish horses. Use of the double bridle during such training should be temporary, however, progress being frequently checked by testing the work on the snaffle. One should be able to ride and train a horse through to the Grand Prix exercises on a plain snaffle bit.

The curb bit has a single unbroken mouthpiece. Its shanks are a lever which, via the curb chain as a fulcrum, puts pressure on both the tongue and the bars of the mouth (this does depend on the size of the port). The curb bit can only be used as a restraining or receiving tool – regulating the rhythm, and helping to maintain the balance in the horse.[11] Therefore the bridoon is added, in order to facilitate control over the bend as well. To ride correctly on the curb alone requires great experience, and the horse must be well prepared and supple as butter.

There are four factors that determine the severity of the curb – the thinner the mouthpiece (bar), the longer the shank, the larger the port, and lastly, the more tightly the curb chain is fitted – the more severe the curb bit.

With the exception of the above-mentioned, no other bits have any place in riding or training in accordance with Classical principles.

Having said this, it is important to add that the issue lies not so much in what we use as *how* we use it. An experienced rider who understands the full ramifications of working the *whole* horse correctly could potentially use more severe bits without sacrificing the quality of the work. But the good rider doesn't really need to use severe bits, and can ride just as well with a plain, mild snaffle bit. The advice for students to use mild bits is certainly not aimed at denying anyone opportunities for advancement. It is, in fact, a far surer guarantee of real progress, because effective horsemanship does not originate at the bit in the first place!

It cannot be sufficiently strongly advised never to punish the horse with the bit. This practice must be considered a gross brutality! It annihilates the horse's confidence in the rider, and is highly destructive to the gaits. If punishment is absolutely necessary, a more effective and less damaging alternative would be to discipline the horse with a smart whack with the stick (see 004: 22).

074 Use of Auxiliary Tack

All of the following auxiliary equipment, which is used to place the horse's head artificially, has no place in the natural training of the horse.

---

[11] With this in mind, it is a sound concept to ride with the reins 'three and one': The left bridoon rein and both curb reins in the left hand, and the right bridoon rein alone in the right hand.

— Draw reins
— Chambon
— Side-reins (other than for longeing)
— Martingales (standing or running)
— German running reins
— Very sharp spurs

On very rare occasions,[12] and then only in the most competent of hands, can side-reins or draw reins be used *briefly* on badly spoiled horses which continually free themselves from the rider's aids by severe tossing of the head; or they can be used to help stabilize horses with particularly wobbly (spaghetti) necks. However, use should be discontinued as soon as possible; these artificial aids are a temporary means to assist the rider in eradicating specific problems. Having said this, frankly, the truly experienced rider never needs to use such auxiliary reins,[13] realizing that they are a 'quick–fix', which do not actually assist in establishing sound, long-term results, and which usually only cover up the symptoms of deeper, more fundamental problems.

Very sharp spurs are unhorsemanlike. The point at which an aid loses its effectiveness and becomes unacceptable is when it starts to cause pain and/or actually damages the horse. ('Where brutality begins, the art desists' – E. von Neindorff.) It is important to interject that punishment, *per se*, has nothing to do with giving aids, and it should *never* cause physical damage. Generally, the spurs should be used to reinforce the sideways-yielding aids. The stick is a far more effective support for the driving aid because it directly initiates the horse's natural desire to flee. The spurs, on the other hand, may cause some horses to withhold their fluid forward motion; they should be used sparingly and discreetly.

---

[12] This means what it says. Everyone far too readily claims their circumstances to be 'rare occasions', until such exceptions become a regular part of their riding and training. It is most sincerely recommended not to fall into this trap.

[13] The author *never ever* uses auxiliary reins (side-reins during longeing excepted) even when retraining seriously spoiled horses.

075 Longeing the Horse

All the principles of riding apply to the longeing as well (035, 036). One needs a well-cultivated eye and an intuitive sense for the horse's energy and motion to be able to influence it favourably and reap the benefit from longeing work. Longeing and in-hand work in general require special skills and talents. Not everyone who can ride well is able to longe well; conversely, some people who have a real knack for working horses from the ground can prove to be no more than mediocre riders. Certainly, having the horse merely twirling around on the longe, usually in too fast a rhythm, is a waste of time, and can even be damaging to the horse's legs.

With regard to the adjustment of side-reins, there are too many variables in daily circumstances, and from horse to horse, to make any definite or pat recommendations. A fairly safe rule-of-thumb, however, is to end up having the horse's head in the correct position (040) when trotting. It is better to have the side-reins a bit too long than too short. It is very important that the handler knows how to match-up the level of impulsion with the level of compression set by the side-reins.

For some young horses, during approximately the first three to six weeks of longeing, the head should be adjusted to face slightly to the outside (sufficiently so that the horse's hind legs continue to track in the path of the front legs). As the horse learns to balance itself, and to use its hindquarter without any sideways evasions of the croup (usually toward the outside), one can gradually make both side-reins equal, and finally change the bend to the inside, on the circle line.

If at any time a horse (regardless of training level) should show resistance against the *inside* side-rein (indicated by looking out), this should not be corrected by shortening the inside rein yet more. The correct solution here is a patient and lengthy one. Both side-reins should be set slightly longer and absolutely equal. The horse should be sent well forward,[14] and coaxed into reaching more with the

---

[14] Take care, however, to keep a reasonably cadenced rhythm. Do not rush the horse off its feet.

outside of its neck and body to fill the outside rein better. Once the horse accepts both side-reins equally then the inside rein may be slightly shortened once again.

The side-reins should be quite long for young horses, and their longeing sessions should always be started and ended with five to ten minutes without side-reins. Make a habit of using either a longeing cavesson or a halter (over the bridle) for all longeing work. Do not attach the line to the bit, as this can unnecessarily inhibit forward flow and, in inexperienced hands, can cause the horse to become tense and distrustful of the bit.

It is best to avoid jerking the horse around with heavy-handed snatches on the line. It is ignorant, brutal and a waste of time. Besides being potentially damaging, it can only cause the horse to become fearful and silly. If the horse is rushing, make the circle smaller for a while until it settles down, then gradually go larger again.

Corrections when longeing

— **If the horse is lugging on the line** this can be corrected best by *standing in one spot*,[15] and repeatedly changing the *quality* of the contact on the line: **close** – open, **close** – open, **close** – open with the fingers. Do not pull back at all, and always end up with a soft, relaxed contact. Remember, horses can only lug when we give them something to lug on. Keep the horse moving fluidly forward.

— **If the horse is making erratic circles, by cutting in** *stand in one spot*. Start by making the circle a bit smaller. The key to success is to correct the horse on the side where it wants to cut *out*, and this will automatically stop it cutting in on the other side of the circle. Here is how it's done: keep the horse **in** on the side where it wants to cut out, while driving it *tactfully*. On the other side, where it wants to cut in, do not drive, do not back up (stand your ground); above all stay relaxed, and ignore the horse's cutting in completely. It will take a few minutes to smooth the circle out and have

---

[15] Steadiness, and regularity of the circle (size and location) are indispensable to success.

the horse become even on the longe line all the way around. Only absolute steadiness and consistency of the handler's position and corrective attitudes will bring success.

General Points

— Be relaxed, calm, and quiet in the middle of the longeing circle. Do not wander around.[16] Keep the contact on the line elastic, light and even, with a relaxed wrist, elbow and shoulder, exactly as it should be during riding.

— Keep the elbow, hand, horse's mouth on a straight line (when looking from the side, or from above). The forearm must become part of the longe line.

— Do not 'lead' (pull) the horse forward with the longe line. Drive it forward with the stick only.

— In longeing, as with riding, it is best to make corrections 90 degrees (a quarter of a circle) ahead of where the trouble spots are.

Uses of equipment

Longeing from the halter or cavesson, without side-reins, bridle or tack, is used for the following reasons:

— The very first longeing sessions for the horse. The horse learns its first obedience, that is, going quietly and steadily around the handler in both directions, without hindrance from tack; this helps to establish a regular rhythm at the trot. The horse learns the basic voice aids.

— As a method of free longeing for any horse, to give simple, controlled exercise.

— Initial retraining for badly spoiled horses.

Longeing from cavesson with a bridle and side-reins:

— Establishes the balance, regularity and stability in the gaits.

— The horse learns that the bit is to be *trusted* and respected;

---

[16] Unless truly capable of walking on a near-perfect circle.

that the bit doesn't do anything so long as it yields through its entire body and searches for a contact on it. The horse quickly teaches itself not to pull against the bit, but to balance itself instead (provided, of course, that the handler does not interfere in any way, and merely ensures that the horse continues to flow forward freely on a regular, smooth circle).

076 Longeing the Rider

Much longeing without stirrups, especially at the trot, is a vital part of acquiring good physical habits and excellence in our riding. It is an opportunity for putting extra effort into correcting specific problems, which is often not as easy to do under ordinary riding conditions off the longe.

Purposes of longeing the rider:
— Rider can concentrate solely on self, gaining self-confidence, and finding balance and harmony with the horse's movements.

— By doing free, playful exercises, rider learns to overcome tensions, and gains suppleness and *independence* of individual body parts; learns how to be well let down past the hips and thighs and therefore settles properly on the seat bones and crotch – the 'triangle' (008).
— Rider attains the correct position, which is an integral part of a good seat, and suitable aiding influences on the horse.

In keeping with the fact that the seat and position should be a wholly functional part in the giving of aids, students should keep the horse moving forward by themselves as much as possible (007).

Which horse should be used to longe the rider?

While longeing beginners or nervous riders, until they become more acquainted with the horse's motion and gain in self-confidence, a reliable, quiet, older horse should be used. As the student becomes more proficient, then more sensitive or energetic horses can be used.

Important: In the first years of training, young horses should be spared this pounding-around on the longe, with riders doing sitting trot without stirrups. It is usually detrimental to the training, and can be damaging to the horse.

Safety points for longeing:

— Have the longe line carefully organized (no knots or twirls). If the horse bolts, and the longe line is badly organized, the line can easily knot firmly onto the hand, causing serious damage.
— *Always wear gloves while longeing!*
— *Always have the bridle reins organized in such a way that the person being longed can use the reins to control the horse if something unforeseen should happen (line breaking, or coming loose; or if the person longeing the horse loses control).*

Reflections VI

— An experienced rider doesn't need to use severe bits; an inexperienced rider certainly shouldn't use them.

— In the truest sense of the word the bit must remain the mediator between horse and rider, upon which neither may pull (neutral territory).

— The riding school should be a place of quiet work. Excessive noise in either the school or around the stables should be avoided.

— The horse should be tacked up carefully, and with properly fitting tack. Carelessness can cause saddle sores or girth galls, or tossing of the head if saddles or bridles are uncomfortable or ill-fitted.

— Tighten the girth gradually, and never over-tighten it, as tensions will be caused in the horse's back; not to mention souring the creature.

— Be gentle while grooming; the horse is not a carpet! Remember, true horsemanship starts on the ground.

— It is not praise for the horse to get huge slaps on the neck or croup. Stroking or patting the neck gently is usually better received by most horses.

— Beginners aren't bad riders, they merely lack experience. The only truly bad riders are usually 'experienced' (in the poorest sense of that word!); those who blatantly and ignorantly bully their horses, while using them as a stage for their own egos.

— Riding students, like horses, need to be brought along within the limits of their own capabilities at any given time. Requesting advanced work (to satisfy the ambitions of the instructor) without an adequate foundation only forces the inexperienced rider into many poor habits – not to mention the needless distress the horse is subjected to under such circumstances.

— 'Always be a friend to the horse's back' (Egon von Neindorff).

Barty. Piaffe. Only through continued judicious exercising in the basics will improvement be realised in this advanced work. Though the quality of the contact is good, and the horse is pleasant in its neck and in expression (accepting), the stiff, unquiet tail indicates physical strain as the hindquarters commence to lower and bear more weight.

CHAPTER VII

The Subject of Photography

077 The Assessment of Horsemanship in Photography

For the experienced eye, a photograph of horse and rider is worth considerably more than a thousand words. Pictures reveal accurately the quality of the performance at the particular moment the shot was taken.

We should certainly not condemn a rider on the strength of one photograph; anyone can have a bad day or moment now and then. The personal value in assessing equestrian photos lies in establishing more clearly in our mind what the true standards of Academic Horsemanship[1] are, thereby becoming more proficient in criticizing our own work, and better equipped to improve it.

To sharpen our perception for judging pictures, frequent practice is essential. If we adhere to a set plan of evaluation, we can avoid the problem of trying to see everything at once, and ending up seeing almost nothing at all.

078 Suggested Sequence in Assessing Photographs

1) General impression.
2) Technical points.
3) Purity of gaits.

[1] Based as objectively as possible on the nature of the horse, as opposed to subjective opinion.

079 General Impressions

Favourable Attributes	**Poor Attributes**
Pleasing	Unattractive, disagreeable
Harmonious	Discordant, incompatible
Balanced	Awkward, disjointed
Elegant	Stiff, affected, uncomfortable
Beautiful, serene, content	Pompous, busy, distressed
Peaceful	Belligerent, adversarial
The apparent ease of the performance	Trying hard, forced

Note: With time and experience we begin to see the 'heart', or the spirit of the moment, and the degree of balance, and above all the flow (or blockage) of the essential 'energy pattern' through the horse and rider. It all begins to waft magically off the page, like incense.

080 Technical Points

(a) Correct position of the horse's head (040).

(b) Sufficient length in the neck.

(c) Flexion of the knee and hock of those legs suspended in the air (depends somewhat on the timing of the photo).[2]

(d) The horse must appear to be 'in front of' the rider (uphill).

(e) Flowing, quiet tail carriage.

(f) Pleasant, content, accepting 'spirited' expression on the horse's face.

(g) Correct position and seat of the rider (see Chapter II).

(h) The pensive, composed, serene, elegant, unforced appearance of the rider.

[2] One should always take into account the individual horse's build, suppleness and degree of training. A green horse, no matter how well ridden, will simply not look as good as a well-trained horse in Medium or Advanced stages of dressage. Also, those horses with a round 'Hackney' motion will generally make far more spectacular photos than those with a flatter 'daisy-cutter' motion. This difference is particularly evident in collected work.

The timing of the shot is similarly pertinent to making a viable judgement. When taken too late, the front foot will already be on the ground. When taken too early, the legs will not be extended forward, or developed, sufficiently to demonstrate the gait to best advantage. Therefore, the well-timed photo shows most clearly the desirable flexion of the knee and hock, and also the amount of leg activity.

081 Purity of the Gaits

(a) Establish which gait is being portrayed.
(b) Check the purity of the gait:
  – walk, 4-beat (053)
  – trot, 2-beat (055)
  – canter, 3-beat (056)
  – rein-back, 2-beat (061)

(c) In extensions, the horse's whole frame must lengthen; *the neck especially needs to be stretched, proportionate to the length of the stride;* the hind legs thrusting forward actively and purely.
(d) In collection, the horse must appear to be going uphill because of a supple back which results in lowered, more engaged hindquarters; flexion of the three major joints of the hind leg should be evident.

Note: In photographs there is little appreciable visual difference between medium and extended trot because the length of the moment of suspension does not show. At the medium trot the horse will already have almost fully extended its legs. That which differentiates the medium trot from the extended trot lies only in a more powerful thrusting-off of the hind legs, resulting in a more pronounced moment of suspension, and therefore a longer stride.

At the extended trot the front leg should point to the place where it will be landing; an exaggerated 'forward–upward' reaching of the forelimbs ('goose-stepping') should be avoided. Ideally speaking, the front feet should not extended beyond an imaginary line drawn along the horse's face to the ground. However, some horses do display great freedom of the shoulder, and thus extend the forelimbs slightly beyond this line. This is acceptable provided that there is still a bend in the knee; that there is no hovering or tension in the gait; and that the requirement of diagonal unison is still fulfilled (055).

These photos portray Atlantis during piaffe work. The cornerstone of correct work lies in the presence of the supple back. These photos illustrate this from, on the one hand (top), a soft stretching and yielding forward and down (the horse's nose should be pointing somewhat more forward) and on the other hand, the supple

deeply bent haunches in the piaffe (bottom left). Compare the height of the tail from the ground with the halt on p96. On the right hand page the horse is shown in a more advanced stage of the training, both in the snaffle and in a double bridle.

Note: *Any deviations from the exact, correct footfall must be deemed to be a deviation from the ideal standard of Academic Riding.*

082 Incorrect Work

Incorrect work invariably manifests itself in distortions of the gaits, usually because of either laziness or tensions. In both instances the horse doesn't step through its back, and lacks the elastic unity between hindquarters and forehand, which originates from forward desire.

Laziness: The horse may seem quite happy and the general appearance pleasant, however, one will be able to detect lagging hindquarters and imbalance in the horse, which drags itself around on the forehand, often boring on the rider's hands, sometimes with the face behind the vertical, and the poll not as the highest point. The horse does not appear uphill or in front of the rider.

Tensions: Almost without exception, tensions start in the horse's back, then manifest themselves in the poll and jaw and in the stiff tail carriage. As a result the horse no longer flexes the joints of its legs, and goes around 'peg-legged'; using its legs only, without the cooperation of a supple, elastic back. Such horses are referred to as 'leg-goers'. The gaits could appear short and choppy, and at times display a hovering quality. The inexperienced observer might find the 'flashy' movement of such tense horses impressive.

083 Signs of Tensions or Incorrect Work

— Incorrect head position (038 a–e; 040).
— Too short a neck in relation to the degree of extension or collection of the gait.

Meteorite. Incorrect work. An over-sped forehand at the extended trot. Note that the right front foot is still on the ground while its diagonal partner (left hind) is already airborne.

Meteorite. Incorrect work. An over-sped hindquarter at the extended trot. The right hind foot has landed long before its diagonal partner, the left front. Such indications of tension can be shown by any horse that is not supple. One's eye must be very sharply developed to be able to see these points while the horse is in motion. Conveniently, the camera captures this split-second disharmony.

A fairly good demonstration of diagonal unison at the extended trot. Note that the gait is in general more elastic. This is shown in particular by the bend in the knee of the front leg. Compare this with upper photos. The rider should not be leaning backwards.

141

— The croup is high; the horse appears to be 'out behind' the rider.
— Impure footfall in the gaits. The legs appear stiff.
— Crookedness.
— Tensions evident in the neck, poll, or jaw.
— Horse's neck broken or kinked at the third vertebra behind the poll.
— The tail-carriage is stiff or swishing.
— The horse's mouth is dry. The lips are opened, snarling.
— An angry, unhappy or frightened, or vacant, dead expression on the horse's face and eyes.
— Poor position of the rider. For guidelines, see Chapter II; and 021–025.
— Any stiffness detected in the rider.
— Rider does not appear to be sitting *in* the horse; a general picture of disharmony and discomfort.
— Rider's facial expression strained.

The Old Masters

In the absence of living examples by which we can guide and rectify our riding (since most riders do not enjoy the opportunity to either see or work with teachers who are truly 'Masters'), we can still benefit greatly from making a regular habit of looking long and patiently at illustrations of the old Masters. Many unspoken essences can be absorbed in this way, and can affect our riding positively. The rarity of photographs of such excellent examples should serve as a warning that we must remain ever-vigilant about the quality of our work, if we ever wish to approach and uphold the ideal by which these Masters measured their performance. Note especially the serenity which emanates from these photographs.

Richard L. Wätjen, medium trot, on Burgsdorff. Beautiful harmony in motion. Enormously impulsive, elastic, and forward.

Epigram

Only a rider who does not deceive himself,
who does not always look for and find excuses for himself,
but rather, who always stands clearly and unerringly
in light of the actual task,
and perseveres with unwavering passion and love for
horses and the art of riding,
can after long, arduous work draw closer to his ideal.
The realization that he has always yet to learn brings the true rider
to dedicate his life to this art.

Richard L. Wätjen.

Richard L.Wätjen, medium canter on Feuerhorn. Note the inclination of the upper body, in perfect dynamic balance with the moment.

Oberbereiter Meixner, canter pirouette left on Favory Ancona. The epitome of collection, bend, and deep flexion of the hindquarters.

Above: *Ernst Lindenbauer, working canter right. Beautiful, uphill, 'carrying' canter. Exemplary position and attitude; note the forward-drawing quality of the front line.*

Opposite top: *Richard L. Wätjen, passage on Burgsdorff.*

Opposite bottom: *Oberbereiter Meixner, passage. The finest example of the 'long front line' of the upper body.*

147

Oberbereiter Meixner, levade.

CHAPTER VIII

Thoughts on the Nature of Art

Nature does not hide her secrets by way of ruse, but because she is so essentially lofty. Albert Einstein

Introduction

The subject of this final chapter has been broached because of the fairly common and indiscriminate use of the title 'The Classical Art of Riding', to describe almost any dressage, irrespective, it seems, of its actual quality. Indeed, not all dressage riding attains to artistic spheres. In the following study, therefore, I have tried to identify those elements which might be deemed essential before a work could be considered art at all.

It may surprise the reader to find that this essay is not restricted solely to Classical Riding, but that it casts its net far afield in search of the most fundamental essences of art in general. This has been done because I believe that all art forms must share a common basis. Thus, if that universal foundation can be delineated, it will possibly help us to see more clearly not only what makes art 'art', but also under what circumstances High School riding could be considered to take its rightful place among aesthetic works of art.

A SHADOW OF ART

In step with Force of forces
Dancing
Work of hands
Entranced
The medium fashioned
To life now trembles
Gift of circumstance.

In mind's deep forest
Self absented
Witness to participant
Transforms
And there among the boughs
Discovers
Such beauty as Truth adorns.

Its strange familiar aires
Composing
Primal Cosmic bars
As the bow of toil
Faint tremor draws
From strings
That play the stars.

By art's elixir now trilling
One
Embraced the Love
That lit the Sun.

The Apostle Philip. Leonardo da Vinci. Study sketch for his fresco 'The Last Supper'.

A View on the Properties of Art

Besides the controversial subjects of religion and politics, few topics come to mind that can elicit more lively discussion than those which tangle with the elusive nature of art. This is particularly so if we consider that the word 'art' appears to have been used to describe almost every human toil, ranging anywhere from Rembrandt's masterpieces to skinning a fish! Well then, we might ask, what actually does constitute art?

Certainly the word 'art', in its broadest sense, could indeed apply to many of mankind's works and products, provided these are of the highest quality. But here, for the sake of analysis, I have divided this topic into two basic categories: functional, and aesthetic art.

Functional or technical art would entail those things which fulfil our practical needs – utensils, instruments, furniture, bridges, buildings, cars, ships, aircraft, and innumerable handicrafts. And, of course, 'art' has also come to imply the craftsman's knack or skill in being able to make or do things extremely well.

Aesthetic or fine art, which is the main subject of this essay, drifts into the metaphysical, cultural realm of life. Under this heading we find sculpture, painting, music, and poetry. Also included would be the performing arts, such as ballet, figure-skating, acting, and Classical Riding. The cultivation and expression of the human spirit is the chief quality of this category. The physical and wholly practical give way to the tenuous and spiritual.

Though functional and aesthetic art have been arbitrarily separated here, a sharp line of division does not actually exist between them. Rather, they could be seen as occupying opposite extremes of an imaginary 'art scale', overlapping and merging into one another imperceptibly, somewhere in the middle, where they combine to form a pleasing whole with both practical and aesthetic appeal: a beautiful dress, building, automobile, hand-painted china, or any artistic ornamentation of practical things.

What might further distinguish aesthetic art from its sibling, functional art?

Is aesthetic art not a work of beauty, an inspired act, through which the artist expresses joy of, and admiration for, the object of

their love? Is it not an affirmation of life: an ultimate statement of 'humanness' generated through the disciplined energy of the whole person – body, mind and spirit? In this ethereal quality not precisely that which separates an ordinary handicraft from a masterpiece: that it transcends the confines of three-dimensional time and space, and finds its reflections deep within archetypal cosmic essences of our being? Are these not the attributes that have conferred to art its timeless quality, whereby it has leaped beyond ideologies, fashions, boundaries and cultures over the ages – making it truly the common idiom of all mankind?

At this point, a question arises as to what qualities a person might need to be able to produce aesthetic art. The short list of basic requirements would surely have to include technical skill, physical dexterity and, most importantly, artistic talent. Let's have a closer look at what talent might be.

Talent is an inborn ability. Undoubtedly, everybody has a degree of talent in some area of the vast spectrum of human activity: athletic, managerial, mechanical, philosophical, just to mention a few. Each endeavour requires its own special aptitude, which must be nurtured and developed if its full potential is to be realized. Lastly, it is clear that talent ranges anywhere from fairly common, mild levels, to the rare orbits of genius.

That talent which pertains to the production of aesthetic art might be measured by the degree of an individual's perceptive sensitivity for, and ability to harmonize with, the physical and spiritual workings of Nature. It follows that one who is gifted with artistic talent will be guided by a gut-feeling or intuitive knowledge: a subconscious spontaneity which synthesises the artist's conscious intentions as the spiritual and material fabric of art are woven into a work of beauty.

The greatest of technical skills without artistic talent would probably result only in a handicraft – technically perfect, yet sterile and lifeless, without any significant qualities beyond its face value. On the other hand, it would be highly improbable – if not impossible – for exceptional art to be produced without technical skill. It is interesting to note, however, that some works which are not entirely technically perfect still radiate considerable aesthetic charm. Notwithstanding this, I personally believe that there would be an inherent danger in taking such a phenomenon as a basic guideline because the concept of 'freedom of expression', taken to the extreme, would surely bring only mediocre results if the artist were erringly to equate this with freedom from discipline. It would appear to me that only the solid mastery of technique, growing side by side with the flowering of talent, enables the artist to manipulate the chosen medium effortlessly, and allows the desired expression to flow, unimpeded by the limitations of technical or physical awkwardness. In this way talent is fully liberated and finds its wings.

When considering those qualities central to good art, none stands out more prominently than beauty. In fact, beauty seems to encompass all other significant aspects of art within itself. Is it not through the evocative power of beauty that we are inspired and uplifted? Surely, a work which lacks this essential element cannot attain the domain of aesthetic art.

Our first impulse might be to consider beauty an entirely subjective matter. Upon closer scrutiny, however, we can discover that it is possible to establish a fairly objective evaluation if we endeavour to seek a guiding authority beyond ourselves.

What is beauty? Beauty finds its origins in the core of the Creator Spirit of the Universe: the furnace of Nature's mighty laws and forces, to which all existence hums in perfect obedience. Its natural precepts and elements have been set down at the birth of time, and exist with or without our recognition or approval. Its constants are always there, waiting for us to discover and understand them.

Beauty is an attribute that cannot be abstracted from the object which possesses it, but must, rather, be wholly intrinsic within it. If something is to be beautiful it must be true to its own nature. That is, it must have a deep-rooted harmony with natural law: be in accord with its environment, and radiate a purity and authenticity from the innermost core of its being. One could say that beauty is synonymous with quintessential harmony and truth. It manifests itself as practical or functional beauty – a well-made utensil or tool; physical beauty – a lovely face or beautiful form, or in graceful, elegant, fluid motion; and last, spiritual beauty – outstanding virtues of personality or character. These forms can be found singly or in any combination with each other.

The nub of our ability to detect beauty lies in an inborn sense for recognizing harmony in Nature. We have this primal intuition because we are as much a part and product of Nature as all the creatures on earth and all the stars in the heavens. One might say we are the reflective molecules of the Universe. We are therefore also inescapably subject to the natural laws that govern both our physical and spiritual existence. It is this basal heritage which affords us the intuitive beacon by which our judgement is guided; provided, of course, it hasn't been clouded by preconceptions or warped by contrived, fossilized doctrine. Truth from the mouth of babes!

These points are not intended to be dismissive about the very real factor of personal taste. Thankfully, beauty manifests itself in many varied ways, enough to satisfy the infinite diversity of individual preference. Yet, only by honing our perceptive awareness and gaining adequate understanding, based on personal experience of specific art forms, will a more mature and objective evaluation develop. This will allow us to recognize and appreciate a broader spectrum of fine art treasures, even though they might not always be to our personal taste. We may, for example, genuinely admire the paintings of seventeenth century Dutch Masters, yet prefer not to have them hanging on our walls at home.

Taking into account the properties of beauty, and the faculties we possess for recognizing it, we can readily see how these need to be an integral and essential part of the production of fine art. Each work should reflect just such deep-rooted accord with Nature's laws. This is embodied in its balance, its purity of rhythm, the harmony of its tonality, the fluidity of its motion, and the excellence of its proportion.

But taking us beyond these measurable qualities, through the deft mediation of the artist, the work must resonate its inherent cosmic truth in the very core of our soul. This inscrutable element, which so grips us, entails the very reason for art's existence – being mankind's fascination with the intricacies of life, and our insatiable desire to come to understand them. It is an expression of our yearning to find harmony with our roots.

This deeper causal aspect exists because, to create a work of fine art demands of us that we come to understand, consciously or intuitively, the nature of both our medium and subject. For unless we work within the structures of the nature of both – being in harmony with their truths – we will surely fail to achieve the higher ideals of artistic expression.

The very act of finding harmony with the nature of one's own specific art form indirectly opens the doors to finding harmony with all of Nature combined. And as the inner eye of our soul recognizes the fundamental truths it beholds, we experience a sublime state, an ecstacy that sets our physical and spiritual senses alight with joy. Through such delightful snippets of insight we come to a better understanding of the nature of life itself, though this might be a wholly intuitive and indefinable insight.

How do these general observations apply to the subject of this book, horsemanship?

In the art of High School riding, as with the other performing arts, such as ballet or ice-dancing, ultimate performances only become possible once harmony is found with the laws of physics that govern the dynamic equilibrium of a moving body. Only then can personal expression be transmitted, to be combined into an exhilarating, fluid performance of beauty in motion.

As riders, however, we have a double duty on our hands. Not only must we develop a refined control over our own mind and body, but we must, through exercising judicious leadership, achieve cooperation from the horse as well. This entails the indispensable aspect of physical unity with the horse, which is unattainable, however, without an initial 'meeting of minds'. The serene melody of spiritual union can only be founded on respect, trust, goodwill, and mutual cooperation. Any strictly technical, physical, or forceful manipulations of the creature can never attain genuinely artistic performances, but rather result only in clever 'handicrafts' at best. The rider should, therefore, strive only to direct or guide. The *apparent* control achieved is, in effect, a true manifestation of the horse's own willingness, through the conditioning and *understanding* it has gained from its training, to comply with the rider's reasonable guiding requests. For it, too, recognizes the universal law which has structured its being, and senses pleasure from working harmoniously with a sensitive, benign rider.

Through wholehearted subjection to the natural laws that govern the horse, mankind's intellect can judiciously contribute the disciplined gymnastic training (that which the horse is incapable of without man's intervention) which develops the creature's athletic potential, whereby it can begin to move with the grace and balance of a dancer while carrying the rider.

Only after many years of relentless searching for and working in accordance with the horse's truths, can an equestrian concert eventually ensue, in which human and creature are joyfully united in purest harmony. The hallmark of such a performance, besides the palpable delight emanating from both horse and rider, lies in the unmistakable suppleness and verve of the movements, which are presented with playful ease – effortlessly 'tossed-in', as it were. This, and only this, when honestly achieved, can be considered to have attained Classical ideals, and can be labelled *aesthetic art*.

We must take care not to be tempted into believing that art is only produced when we are riding the advanced movements. Art can exist at any level, regardless of the simplicity or complexity of the work. A Grand Prix ride can most definitely lack any vestige of art. Conversely, a first-level ride can embrace art fully. An analogy can be drawn between horsemanship and a sketch or oil painting. A good sketch (rudimentary levels of riding) is a skeleton which must contain all vital essences of the subject matter. And the oil painting (the advanced levels of riding) is an expansion in the dynamic range of those basic essences through the added dimensions of colour, hue and tonality.

To be an artist is to answer an irresistible calling. It is not motivated by ambitions for notoriety or material riches, nor does it yield to the pressures of popular demand. It is a dedication of one's life to the simplicity of the daily task, born of a singular, invincible urge to attain excellence through the fulfilment of a talent that cannot be denied. This is unfalsifiable, for only in the truth of one's product – its honesty and good quality – lies the foundation of one's authority to be called an artist.

When the artist escapes all bonds, and soars into the spaceless halls of unselfconsciousness, the finest of works are born. When fleeting glimpses of creative inspiration, as though of their own accord, opportunely coincide with flowing moments of physical skilfulness, spirit and matter merge, and are transformed into a delicate substance which radiates a life of its own – a life which is greater than the participants involved – it becomes a celebration of all Creation.

Ever a catalyst to thought and searching, art teases and awakens our curiosity as it exposes the compelling intricacies of universal workings. And so we are drawn unwittingly into the wonderous gardens of life's mysteries, when we are touched by the ineffable and the intangible – it is art.

Photo by J.G. Herbermann.

Closing Thoughts

Just what is in store for Classical riding in these times? Ours is indeed a trying era, one in which we are incessantly accosted by frivolity, numbed by sensationalism, and seduced by the easy voice of instant gratification. We are lead to believe that solutions are readily and painlessly available for all of our problems and dreams. We have become so crafty at producing imitations of every kind that we have become blunted, and no longer appear to miss things of real value. Thus we have gradually isolated ourselves from the laws of Nature, and fail to notice our disharmony with it. So long as things *look* good, that's all that seems to matter!

The art of riding does not find its home easily in such modern-day philosophy. The horse doesn't understand how to be anything other than itself. Its nature will not be hurried. Yet, God only knows, the wiles of humanity respect no bounds. For centuries riders have attempted to find short-cuts to training the horse, and have forced the creature into taking on baseless *symptoms* of correct work, with blatant indifference for its well-being. Unavoidably, those who partake in such error fall victim to their own contrivances, and begin to believe that these perversions of the horse actually result in a valid product. The connoisseur, however, looks straight through the shallow glitter of the pretender's 'High School movements', and recognizes the tense or broken gaits, and either the over-stressed nerves, or the soulless obedience of the horse's defeated spirit.

Let us dare to look the fact straight in the eye. Regardless of what we think are our real or imagined qualifications in the saddle, not any one of us – neither this author, nor any riding instructor, nor all of the Masters past or present – can lay rightful claim to the title 'Horseman' unless we have learned to subject – no, *surrender* – ourselves unconditionally to the nature of the horse. If the horse does not ratify our daily work as being acceptable to it, or if it does not genuinely reflect in its physical and spiritual presence that it has become truly more beautiful because of our intervention,[1] our work is, simply put, not up to Classical standards.

What refinement we must cultivate in order to earn the right to help in the development of the equine ballerina. It is a grave responsibility indeed. One which foremost requires of us that we humble ourselves in the sanctuary of the horse. Let us therefore put aside all petty self-interest, and all work that is not friendly or considerate to this most noble of creatures, and build our horsemanship and our lives, with which it is fully entwined, on substantial fundamental values. For only from such a sound basis can we fully explore the dynamic breadth of this subject, and forge the coveted equestrian union without in any way diminishing the most beautiful aspect of being human for the rider, and of being and remaining fully equine for the horse.

The horses will ever remain our true and ultimate judges; let us always listen to them.

---

[1] Indicated by its mental calmness and acceptance, and the correctness of its muscular development which blossoms through its supple, active, balanced, and pure gaits (068, 069 and Chapter 7).

Recommended Reading

— *Riding Logic*, Wilhelm Müseler.
— *Horsemanship*, Waldemar Seunig.
— *Dressage Riding*, Richard L. Wätjen.

Historically significant texts
— *Gymnasium des Pferdes*, Steinbrecht.
— *Le Manège Royale*, A. de Pluvinel.
— *École de Cavalerie*, de la Guérinière.
— *Horsemanship*, Xenophon.
— *Die Reitkunst im Bilde*, Ludwig Koch.

Index

Author's index to key issues within text. The reference numbers in plain text denote the relevant sub-heading. Sub-headings are numbered sequentially throughout the book. Actual page numbers are given in bold italic.